MW01493031

WISDOM
of the
DYING

LESSONS IMPARTED
TO A PANDEMIC PHYSICIAN

Hamza Abbasi, MD

ISBN: 978-1-963569-83-4 (Hard Cover)
         978-1-963569-84-1 (Soft Cover)

Abbasi. Hamza.

Edited by: Amy Ashby

Published by Warren Publishing
Charlotte, NC
www.warrenpublishing.net
Printed in the United States

To my sister, Javairia,
who taught me the courage it takes to be kind.
You are my hero.

Table of Contents

Introduction

On Wednesday mornings in our academic hospital, we have a conference called "Grand Rounds." As the radiance from a golden sunrise shines through the large windows, illuminating the room for another dawn on the wards, physicians of all different fields and specialties file into the auditorium to take their seats. The older docs with white coats, their gray hair thinning with experience, take out leather-bound notebooks, while us greener physicians boot up our laptops. A doctor in a formal suit, one of the resident physicians, takes the stage to go through a complex or unique case that highlights intricate clinical reasoning or a cutting-edge procedural technique in their field.

The Grand Rounds conference has been a staple of teaching hospitals all over the world for over a century. It began in the late 19th century at the storied Johns Hopkins School of Medicine in Baltimore, where medical students would crowd around a patient's bed to observe legendary clinician Sir William Osler (known among doctors as "the father of modern medicine") as he examined that week's most complex patient for the first time. They'd watch in awe as he would arrive at a diagnosis within minutes through careful history-taking and precise physical examination with skill and veracity that would put House, M.D. to shame. Mind you, this was a hundred years before the invention of the MRI scanner.

Times have changed since Sir William Osler's era. Medicine has transitioned from a paternalistic practice to one of shared decision-making between a health-care provider and their patient. The expansion of medical education institutions as well as the wide array of medical specialists now present in the hospital has shifted Grand Rounds from the bedside to the auditorium. The old-school docs will tell you how, for decades, Grand Rounds has consisted of the on-call resident physician presenting the most complex patient using a carousel slide projector and chalkboard. Nowadays, the hum of the carousel slide projector has been replaced with sleek Microsoft PowerPoint presentations and high-resolution screens displaying MRI and CT scans.

Throughout the decades, despite the ever-evolving technology and culture, the one constant of Grand Rounds has been resident physicians presenting patients after admitting calls—with dreams of following in the footsteps of Sir William Osler.

Grand Rounds gives us the chance to take an hour out of our busy morning to learn from the providers from all over the hospital. The elders share their wisdom acquired from decades of clinical work on the wards. The recent graduates share new evolving methodologies to more efficiently tackle problems. Surgeons and proceduralists share novel surgical approaches with better outcomes. And the cardiologists and nephrologists argue about which organ is most important. Wednesday morning's Grand Rounds is one of the many reasons I love working at an academic hospital.

Summer 2020, I took the elevator up to the lecture hall. The hallway was deserted, and the double doors, which were usually propped wide open, were closed. There was a single sheet of paper taped on them, with the words: "Conferences have been canceled, providers caring for surging COVID admissions."

I graduated medical school and became a doctor in early 2020. When I began working as an internal medicine resident physician, I could not have imagined that my early career would end up being defined by a global pandemic.

You see, I (like many other doctors and, I suspect, many of you) had anticipated that early efforts in social distancing and strict hygiene would curb the spread of COVID-19. Our hope was that through aggressive public health efforts and social movements, the pandemic would end before it ever really started in the United States. I recall an email from an infectious disease colleague saying that if things went according to plan, we'd "be able to return to normal in late 2020."

How naive we were.

COVID cases would of course then proceed to skyrocket exponentially over the next year. Before I knew it, caring for COVID patients in the hospital was what I lived and breathed (through an N95). In the midst of the pandemic surges, I cared for patients in several clinical settings, depending on the need at the time, including the Intensive Care Unit (ICU), hospital wards, and urgent care clinics.

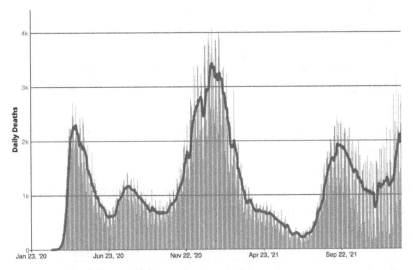

1

Daily Trends in Number of COVID-19 Deaths in the United States Reported to CDC

During that time, before there was a vaccine widely available, approximately one out of every seven individuals with COVID we'd admit to the hospital would die.[2] The sudden tsunami of COVID hospital admissions meant I was exposed to death on the daily.

I had the honor of intimately getting to know so many, many of whom would die in my arms a few days to weeks later. I observed that while on their deathbeds, some of my patients were ready for death, while others were not. Among both of these groups, I began to discern common trends. Many of my patients who were ready for death had common mindsets, principles, and qualities they had lived their lives by. Many of my patients who were not ready for death had common remorse, pitfalls, and regrets.

Over the past few years, I carefully documented these trends and the life lessons that dying patients have imparted upon me. My hope is that the wisdom of those who have suffered through the crucible of sickness can help instill more meaning, purpose, and happiness into our own lives.

Through this book, I will share stories of patients who exemplify the most common lessons expressed at death. These lessons are shaped by the experiences of physicians from across the country at various hospitals and health care institutions battling the COVID pandemic. Each of these chapters is inspired by patients and doctors who have changed my life, and my hope is that you too will benefit from their experiences in life and death.

The teachings they impart are those I have seen in hundreds of patients who have met death, but I anticipate that through sharing the experiences and stories of a few, these lessons can be better illustrated and understood.

I will also include relevant scientific research from the fields of medicine, neuroscience, and psychology that may support (or rebut) the perspectives presented. As someone with degrees in neuroscience and medicine, I am passionate about the intersection between scientific research and humanistic medical care.

Of course, everyone's life is different. We all have different experiences, environments, and feelings. The human experience is a disparate and varied tapestry. What has worked for the patients I have met may not work for you. Although I anticipate that most of these lessons are universally applicable, regardless of whether you instill each one into your life or not, there is wisdom in knowing the experiences of others.

Chapter 1

Become acquainted with death
before death comes for you.

Even in his weakened and sick state, Captain Greg had a formidable presence. The ninety-year-old man's face had a scar crossing his right eye. In my head, I imagined that it was a war wound of some heroic act from an action scene, though I did not think it proper to ask him how he got it. The scar, paired with his gray stubble, sharp blue eyes, and gruff voice, made me think when first meeting him that one could not have cast a better war hero for a movie.

When he first came to the emergency department, he was admitted with a rash and fatigue. He was quite an active man, especially for his age, but lately had been feeling very tired. After the rash showed up, he didn't think too much of it, but he decided to, as he told me, "get it checked out, you know, just in case it's COVID. But I probably just need to sleep better. Fourth of July weekend is always quite hard for me because of the PTSD."

Vague symptoms, such as fatigue or mild rash, are common reasons for presentation to an urgent care or emergency department. These symptoms have a very broad differential diagnosis (shoptalk for developing a list of medical conditions that could be causing the patient's presentation).

Almost always, the etiology is identified as something providers will call "benign," which indicates that the underlying cause is less likely to be from a life-threatening disease, such as cancer, and will usually go away on its own. Nonetheless, it is important to rule out specific causes, as well as obtain objective laboratory data, in order to decide whether a patient needs to be admitted to the hospital.

Over the course of the next few hours, as we worked up a differential and started running some diagnostic tests and labs, I got to know Mr. Greg. With pride, he shared stories of the gallantry of his platoon. He regaled us with tales of bravery and living a mission-driven life in service of others. With sadness in his eyes, he shared the emotional burden of seeing his comrades fall in front of him. He expressed the pain that comes from immense loss.

"We all went in with the mindset that we were ready to sacrifice our lives for the mission. But you don't realize the gravity of death until you've seen it with your own eyes. I did not realize how precious and fragile life was until my friend died in my arms." His eyes welled up with tears as he talked to me.

As the test results began to pop up, his COVID test came back positive. Strangely, his symptoms actually appeared to not be a direct result of the viral infection, but it seemed as if some third process was at play that was provoked by the COVID infection.

As the remainder of the results came in, it was clear that his symptoms were due to a very serious immune reaction called DRESS syndrome. "DRESS" stands for "drug reaction with eosinophilia and systemic symptoms," and "eosinophilia" indicates there are an abnormal amount of a specific type of immune cells (eosinophils) present in the body. Such reactions are often characterized by an extensive skin rash. Captain Greg had started a new gout medication a few weeks ago that was thought to be the culprit.

What makes this condition particularly dangerous is that one's internal organs can become involved. Liver, kidney, lung, and heart injury can be seen in severe forms of the disease. The mortality rate among patients with DRESS is estimated to be roughly 10 percent.[3]

In DRESS syndrome, like in many other diseases, it is our own body's response to the external stimulus, rather than the stimulus itself, that causes the damage. Our body increases production of immune cells, which are usually designed to fight infections. These cells start inflaming one's own body.

There is a sort of poignant symbolism in that it is our own response to the world rather than the world itself that causes the devastating symptoms of many diseases of both physical and mental health. I use this parallel to emphasize the legitimacy and consequence of mental health to my patients. There has historically been a social stigma against psychological diseases. But the mind attacking itself is just as legitimate as the body's immune system attacking itself. You wouldn't tell someone with lupus that it's their own white blood cells attacking their body and they should just focus on the good white blood cells.

Captain Greg and I reflected on this parallel. He had faced a similar stigma when his mental health suffered after he completed a mission where he experienced a large amount of mental trauma. Fortuitously, he had a commanding officer who encouraged him to seek the help he needed. His commanding officer at the time had made a similar comparison to legitimize it just as any other disease.

"When I see a fellow soldier experience physical trauma, I call in medical support. Soldiers experiencing mental trauma need support with the same level of urgency," the captain said.

We immediately started him on the appropriate therapy to counter the immune effects. The mainstay of treatment for these types of diseases is using a class of drugs called corticosteroids (which are different from anabolic steroids—you'd be surprised at how many times I have to clarify that for patients). This is a rather crude approach, as corticosteroids work by reducing the amount and efficacy of circulating immune cells. So it's rather like using a broadsword than a scalpel, as every function of these immune cells gets affected, causing one to be prone to side effects, such as infections for example. There is ongoing research on current and new immunosuppressive agents, which will hopefully augment or replace steroid treatment completely one day.

Over the next day, Captain Greg initially got a bit better. His rash receded. But as the week went on, the progress he had made was offset, and the labs measuring his organ function began to tank. It started as an uptick in his liver enzymes and creatinine (a lab that measures kidney function), but it slowly progressed into almost the entire metabolic lab panel being abnormal. At the rate he was progressing, it appeared as if all his organs would fail within a week.

Patients like Captain Greg always serve as a humbling reminder that no matter how simple a patient's presenting symptoms are, there can always be an insidious underlying disease. This was a lesson I learned early on in the first COVID surge of the pandemic, as I'd have many patients come in with just a cough, fever, and scratchy throat. The infection would progress swiftly, and five days later, they'd be on a ventilator. Their quick clinical deterioration reminds us that tomorrow is not promised to anyone.

Breaking bad news to a patient is something that had become almost a part of my daily workday in the era of COVID. Much like a surgical procedure, it requires a steady hand to guide the approach in a manner that incorporates compassion and respect. We carefully monitor patients and loved ones' subtle expressions and cues to guide our technique. It's such an important skill that there is a whole lecture series in medical school on breaking bad news. I try hard to always do so in an empathetic and emotionally present manner.

I remember the first time I told a patient they were going to die. I was in medical school. I cried as soon as I exited the patient room. As the first tear rolled down my cheek, I felt the tight, cold grasp around my arm of the resident physician who was teaching me. She yanked me out of the hallway and into the workroom.

"We don't do that," she hissed callously. "We're professionals who do what needs to be done. Patients cry. Not us."

I nodded, dried my eyes, and got back to work.

At the time, what she said made sense to me. It is my role to be a comforting presence to patients, not the other way around. However, over the last few years, I have found that suppressing or ignoring one's own emotional state has a counterintuitive effect on the level of empathy one can put into their care. Rather, being emotionally present in a professional manner helps form a compassionate, empathetic doctor-patient relationship, that in turn results in high-quality health care for the patient and a more fulfilling career for the doctor.

Still, I worry that the sheer number of times I have had to have the dreaded conversation of mortality due to the COVID pandemic has made the conversation, despite my best efforts, almost formulaic. Many of my colleagues in medicine and nursing describe this as a major contributing factor to burnout during the era of COVID.

I always make sure to sit next to the patient before telling them their prognosis. I approach cautiously, first empathetically seeing how much they know and what they're expecting. I will often gently hold their hand or their shoulder if appropriate.

The second step is what is known as "firing a warning shot," which is usually done by saying something akin to "unfortunately the results were not what we were expecting." I use their reaction to gauge how I will frame the rest of the conversation as well as to prepare them for the point.

Lastly, I gently tell them the diagnosis and what it means. It is important that when doing so, one does not sugarcoat the implications. If it is a terminal illness, then patients need to know the usual clinical course so they can plan their life accordingly.

When I entered the room, Captain Greg was sitting on his chair, facing the window. He was watching a flock of crows flying outside. I pulled up a chair and sat next to him. He gave me a nod and a soft smile, which I returned. We sat in silence for a few seconds, looking out at the horizon through the window. I broke the silence.

"Mr. Greg, we received the results of the test that we discussed this morning."

I paused as he turned to face me. We had discussed the implications of the potential results this morning, but I still wanted to gently give the difficult diagnosis.

"Unfortunately, the results were not what we were hoping for."

Before I could say another word, he weakly grasped my shoulder with his thin hands. I felt the warmth of his hand through my white coat.

A tear fell down his right cheek as he said, "Son, I have already been acquainted with death. I was younger than you are when I first had a friend fall in front of me. Since then, I have seen death come for many. Many friends have died in my arms, and I've been privy to many final thoughts and breaths. I've known that death could come at any time and have lived a purpose-driven life in anticipation of that. The only surprise for me is that it has taken so long to embrace me."

Patients react very differently to their imminent demise. Some patients or family members react with anger, often directed at the provider. This, unfortunately, was a common reaction during the COVID-19 pandemic, where large amounts of misinformation sowed distrust in the health-care professions. I had one patient's spouse throw a water bottle at me, tell me they didn't believe me, and then proceed to ask me why I wasn't giving the patient bleach when I tried to explain that their spouse's condition was worsening due to COVID.

Other patients react with immense grief, which of course is quite understandable. I find that being a comforting presence for these patients so they know they're not going through this process alone is exceptionally important.

Captain Greg's reaction was rare, although I have seen a handful of patients react like him over the past couple years. It is not that he was not sad—he absolutely was. He would tell me about all of his grandchildren, describing how he would miss them immensely and how he was distraught that he would likely not be able to attend his granddaughter's wedding.

It is rather that he was *ready*. He noted that due to his profession, he had significant and frequent exposure to death, which served as a constant reminder that death was coming.

Everyone *knows* that they will die one day, but it is not something on our minds every day. We may live our day-to-day conveniently forgetting this inevitable fact, and then days add up to years and before we know it, our life is gone.

Captain Greg never forgot that death would one day come for him. He lived every day with this fact in mind. This acceptance drove him to live a life of *purpose*. He sought out meaningful experiences with his loved ones and did not delay in doing the deeds he knew he'd regret pushing off if he did not make it to tomorrow. For Captain Greg, *purpose* meant being a dedicated husband and father, and he savored every one of the precious moments he had with his family. His "acquaintanceship" with death led him to cherish life.

And when death came for him, it was no stranger to him.

Captain Greg was exposed to death in a manner few of us will be, simply by nature of his profession, thus illustrating a dramatic example of the importance of *knowing death*. I have observed similar conscientiousness of death in patients in professions with similar exposure to death, such as health-care workers, first responders, and military members.

I had a patient who was a graveyard worker. I cared for him in the very beginning of the pandemic when he was hospitalized with COVID. He shared with me that because he buried those who passed away every day, he was constantly reminded of his own mortality. Although this caused him some degree of distress when he first started his job, he quickly came to terms with the finite nature of life.

He found that because of this reminder, he lived his life with an increased sense of purpose. He looked to see what brought him happiness, notably spending time with his family and volunteering in his community, and he focused on allocating his time toward those activities. He found that as a result of this shift in thinking, he felt happier.

When he died, he too was ready for death, just as Captain Greg was.

However, such extreme exposure to death is not necessary. Many patients who either died or came near death during the COVID pandemic had similar familiarity with death, but had "normal" jobs.

A patient I care for in my clinic occasionally volunteers in a hospice center so that she could never forget the inevitable end that comes for us all. She notes that doing so gives us a certain perspective about what is important and helps live her life in a meaningful way so that she will be ready when her time comes.

A colleague of mine meditates daily and intentionally contemplates death and mortality while meditating to achieve a similar perspective.

One of my patients is a rather eccentric college professor who has an app on her phone that gives her a daily reminder: "You will die someday."

After he was diagnosed with prostate cancer, Nobel Laureate Archbishop Desmond Tutu said, "When you have a potentially terminal disease, it concentrates the mind wonderfully. It gives a new intensity to life. You discover how many things you have taken for granted: the love of your spouse, the Beethoven symphony, the dew on the rose, the laughter on the face of your grandchild."[4]

Of course, life itself is a "terminal disease," as it is an inevitable fact that we all must die someday. Psychology of awareness of one's mortality is a fascinating area of ongoing research, and many findings support Captain Greg's attitude. Researchers at the University of Georgia point out that acknowledgment of one's mortality can be a catalyst for personal growth: "Acknowledgment of death can be unpleasant, but it can also serve as a roar of awakening."[5]

This practice is present in many spiritual traditions as well. A patient of mine, whom you will meet in a few chapters, is a practicing Buddhist and taught me about Maranasati, which is the Buddhist meditation practice of always knowing that one's death can happen at any time.[6] She showed me pictures of Buddhist meditation halls that had depictions of skeletons throughout to help the monks be mindful of death as they meditated.

Similar ideas are found in Abrahamic religions as well. For example, I once observed the hospital chaplain discussing with a Muslim patient how Islam encourages humanity to be mindful of the temporary nature of life so they can focus on spiritual growth and live purposefully.[7] He noted that when asked by a pupil, "Who is the wisest?" Muhammad said, "Those who remember death often and have best prepared for it."[8]

With the extensive mortality rate of the COVID-19 pandemic, I observed that those who were prepared at the final chapter of their lives were ones who had taken some action to know death. They did so through actions that fostered consciousness of their own mortality, such as mindfulness, volunteering, and spirituality. They instilled this thinking into their daily lives, which resulted in a prioritization in life such that they did not have any regrets in death.

In contrast, those most unprepared at death were those who had not ever taken the time to consider their mortality and were thus ambushed by it, resulting in regret and despair. They had this perspective of life forced upon them at death's door, harshly shining light on how they wished they would have lived their life differently.

I cared for a patient during the Omicron surge who came to the emergency room with a cough and was found to have COVID. He was unvaccinated, as he had refused to get the COVID vaccine due to misinformation propagated on social media websites.

"I'm only seventy-seven. I figure what's the harm if I hold off on the vaccine?" he told me when I first met him.

The infection progressed extremely rapidly in him. Although his breathing continued to worsen, he still did not consider that his life was in jeopardy. When he began requiring a high-flow nasal cannula, a higher level of oxygen support, I discussed with him that if his breathing continued to worsen, he would need to be intubated.

"You have my permission to do that if you need to, but you won't have to. I'll be fine after a couple days when the virus runs its course. I won't be dying for a while. Don't worry, kid," he told me whenever I broached the subject.

The oxygen support he needed increased over the next few days, and slowly his expression changed from indifference to horror. By the end of the week, he was on the verge of needing to be intubated and connected to a ventilator. I can still picture his pale face and wide eyes as he grabbed my scrub top and pleaded with me to save him as he struggled to breathe.

"I can't die! I haven't ever even thought that I'd die! You have to make sure I live!" he begged me while agonizing with every breath. "I still have so much to do! If I die now, what has it been for? I wish I had thought about dying before it came to this."

I tried to tell him words of reassurance and kindness and held his hand as he was intubated. Unfortunately, he died two weeks later as his heart went into a fatal rhythm from the stress of fighting the infection.

Sadly, this reaction is common among patients, particularly those who face their death at a relatively young age. Many older patients get to know death through the passing of their friends or siblings, so they're more likely to have some degree of mental preparedness for their own mortality.

Studying the experiences of both those who were prepared and those who were unprepared when faced with their own mortality can teach us the importance of knowing death while you are living.

Stoic philosopher Seneca wrote, "You live as if you were destined to live forever, no thought of your frailty ever enters your head, of how much time has already gone by you take no heed. You squander time as if you drew from a full and abundant supply, though all the while that day which you bestow on some person or thing is perhaps your last."[9]

Death comes for us, regardless of whether we choose to acknowledge its impending nature. Our preparedness will dictate how ready we are when the time comes.

Chapter 2
Find meaning in a life with others.

By all accounts, Mr. Kensington had a very impressive appearance when I first met him. I remember thinking he had the look and manner of the quintessential Fortune 500 CEO with a hint of old money. Everything about his outfit and demeanor was proper and respectable, thank you very much. He had neatly combed salt-and-pepper hair, a suit with silver cuff links, and a bold red tie with a matching red-and-black Rolex on his left arm. A class ring adorned his hand with an Ivy League crest. He spoke in the sort of posh Connecticut accent you'd picture someone with his appearance would have.

He came into the urgent care clinic due to a mild cough and headache that had been increasingly bothering him over the past couple of days. When I stepped into the room, he was far more interested in telling me his life story rather than his symptoms. I told him that his COVID test was positive and his oxygen levels were low and that he would need to be admitted to the hospital. He only took a second to acknowledge understanding before going back to telling me all about his life.

As an eighty-five-year-old technology company executive, he was chock-full of life experiences that he tried to share with anyone who'd listen. He described his life as rungs on a ladder that he had climbed in order to become the success that he was today.

"My father instilled upon me the importance of achievement in order to keep climbing up in life," he recalled.

When he was in high school, he was determined to get into an Ivy League school like his father. After his admission to Yale—much to his Harvard alumnus father's dismay, he chortled—he was determined to gain entry into the college's elite secret societies. At the end of freshman year, he was able to join the most elite society on campus.

"I've sworn to not share the details of our activities!" he said with a wink and a grin.

I nodded with a polite smile as I tried to get back to listening to his lungs with my stethoscope.

After obtaining his degree in computer science, he went on to land a job at one of the nation's top technology companies while also obtaining his MBA.

"You have to always keep focus. While everyone else was out socializing and partying, I was busy working. Making sure I got to the next rung."

He reminded me of a prosperity gospel motivational speaker.

And climb the rungs he did.

Every time I spoke with Mr. Kensington, he'd regale me with the next chapter in his story of how he climbed up the ranks to where he was now. Sliding open the door to his room was like queuing up another episode of the TV show that was Mr. Kensington. His eyes glowed with a sharp intensity as he earnestly recounted stories from his college days or corporate life. Mr. Kensington certainly had a flare for the dramatic, describing every meeting like a life-or-death situation.

Typically, whenever someone is admitted into the hospital, we ask that person if there is someone they would like their physician to update. It could be difficult to regularly update patients' families, particularly during the COVID-19 pandemic surges when we were already overworked as it was, but we tried our best to call patients' families every day if they asked us to.

I found that this was particularly important during the worst surges of the pandemic, when visits to the hospital were severely limited. Family members relied on doctors and nurses to update them on how their loved one was doing, particularly when the patient was in a state where they could not speak to them over the phone. Health-care workers found themselves to be the singular channel of information and communication between patients and their loved ones. This, alongside the natural anxiety of having a loved one in the hospital during a time of such fear in health care, made this communication an exceptionally meaningful, albeit emotionally exhausting, aspect of our job.

When I asked Mr. Kensington if there was someone he wanted me to update, his ever-present smile faltered for a brief second. The glow from his eyes softened to a look of sadness.

"No, that's okay, son. Much appreciated, but I'll manage that."

We also always ask who the patient's *durable power of attorney* (DPOA) is, as it is important for the medical team to know who would make decisions on behalf of the patient if the patient was unable to do so. This is commonly the patient's spouse, child, or close friend.

"I never got to do the whole wife-and-kids thing. It takes a lot of sacrifice to get to the point I have, I tell you!"

It was the first time I heard the unwavering enthusiasm in his voice replaced by a tinge of regret. The moment was brief, but the tone did not go unmissed by his nurse who gently squeezed his arm before going back to hanging his medications.

He quickly switched back to his trademark enthusiasm. He looked up at me with a big smile.

"I tell you what, though—I need you to do everything to keep me alive. No matter what it takes. I still have a lot that I need to do."

During the era of COVID, it has become standard practice to discuss a patient's preference regarding whether they would like to be intubated whenever they are admitted to the hospital. This is known as discussing their *code status,* and it does not impact any aspect of the standard care they will receive during their hospitalizations. Rather, it refers to whether they will undergo advanced cardiovascular life support (such as compressions, shocks, and emergent medications) should their heart stop beating and whether they will be intubated (which refers to putting a breathing tube into their throat) and connected to a ventilator if they are unable to maintain oxygen levels despite using every other therapy.

Every doctor, regardless of the field, has to be certified in Advanced Cardiovascular Life Support (ACLS), which refers to the guidelines of immediate response to a patient experiencing a cardiac arrest. But research shows that most people overestimate the effectiveness of CPR and ACLS, which may be due to how it is presented as an emergent fix in TV shows. According to the Institute of Medicine, chances of surviving a cardiac arrest outside of a hospital with CPR is 6 percent.[10] The American Heart Association's research indicates that even if someone has a cardiac arrest in the hospital, surrounded by doctors and nurses, only 12 percent of people make it to hospital discharge.[11] Importantly, that does not account for how their brain function is at time of discharge. And on top of that, these statistics are for everyone in the hospital. The survival rates are far lower in the elderly and those with chronic conditions. Those who survive codes often live with significant morbidity.[12]

On my first day of medical school roughly a decade ago, they ushered all of the newly minted medical students out of the humid Chicago summer into the great hall of Northwestern University's medical school. Bronze statues of historic figures in medicine stood alongside the grand arches of the building, giving the room an exalted feeling.

Robotic dummies were spread out throughout the hall, and we learned how to use the patient's electrical monitor to determine which medication to give and when to shock them. Looking back, it was an enjoyable day, quite juxtaposed to the severity of the dire situation we were learning to respond to. We were day-one student doctors who had not yet seen a single patient, let alone been exposed to the grim, harsh realities of caring for dying patients.

I now know that ACLS can be a brutal medical procedure. The patient has *already died,* and the aim is a last-ditch attempt at bringing them *back to life.* Chest compressions, when done correctly, typically break the patient's bones. Lungs can collapse. Depending on the emergent procedures needing to be done, blood can get everywhere. High-voltage shocks administered to the body cause all the muscles to briefly contract. And if one survives ACLS, the lack of oxygen to the patient's brain can sometimes cause a significant decline in function.

Of course, being "Full Code" may be the right decision for the patient. For many, if not most, patients in the hospital, this protocol certainly makes sense. But in patients who are quite elderly and have multiple chronic conditions, the chance of surviving a code with any quality of life becomes increasingly minimal. Nevertheless, code status is a decision made by the patient after a comprehensive and careful conversation with their health-care provider.

As physicians, when we discuss a patient's code status when they are admitted to the hospital, we do our best to make sure they are making a fully informed decision. That can mean that if the chances they will survive a code are minimal, either due to their age or chronic conditions, we explain this to them. This can be a difficult conversation to have, as it means bringing the patient's mortality to the forefront and pointing out that in addition to the ultrasmall chance they survive the code, they will most likely have very severe brain damage requiring significant support from their family for basic human bodily functions.

Mr. Kensington had a severe version of a chronic lung disease called COPD. His disease was so advanced that he required significant oxygen support even at home. This had been worsened considerably by a lifetime of regular smoking. The severity of his disease alongside the nature of the infection meant that realistically, if he were intubated, the chance of being able to eventually remove the breathing tube was almost zero.

As I broached the topic, Mr. Kensington was not having any of it. He turned away in defiance at the topic of his mortality. Attempts at informing him or trying to confer were met with his usual enthusiasm bit by bit being replaced by brazen spite. He had never before considered himself as fallible and the idea of his demise was quite foreign to him.

"As I said, do anything and everything to keep me breathing. If my heart stops, I insist that everything be done. I'm not done with life."

We had our orders.

Over the next two days, Mr. Kensington's sunny demeanor was slowly replaced with a combination of exhaustion and desperation as his breathing worsened. Once, as I checked in on him, he looked particularly depressed. The bright glow in his eyes had been supplanted by a murky twinkle on the verge of being extinguished.

"I have no family. All my friends I know through business. But they must be very busy since they have not been able to ask me how I'm doing."

By the end of his second day in the hospital, he was at maximum levels of a high-flow nasal cannula. I went to his room to examine him after getting paged that his oxygen levels were borderline and dropping.

His eyes were wide when I entered the room. He grabbed me when I came close, every movement causing him to completely lose his breath.

"I ... cannot ... die ... I ... am ... not ... ready!" He took deep breaths in through the high-flow machine between every word, barely able to get them out.

The oxygen monitor began beeping loudly.

Seventy-four percent oxygen saturation levels.

I gathered the procedural supplies needed to intubate him and called the ICU team so that he could be transferred to the ICU and connected to a ventilator.

Up until the very moment we inserted the tube into his mouth, I tried to comfort him. To this day, I can picture his wide eyes looking up at me. All of a sudden, his cold hand grabbed the front of my scrubs like a claw, pulling me close as he breathlessly pleaded with me to give him a few more years of life. I suddenly felt frigid despite the three layers of PPE, and a shiver ran down my back.

"Just a few more years! I can't die now!"

Of course, such power is beyond even the most gifted medical provider.

"I am so alone. I feel like such an old fool. Why did I spend so much time at work instead of making friends?"

I did not know how to answer. My tongue felt trapped in my mouth, and I was at a loss for words, so I just held his hand as the tube was inserted and he was connected to the ventilator. As the sedative took effect, the desperation on his face was replaced with sleep.

Mr. Kensington remained on the ventilator for two weeks. Despite every therapeutic measure, his lungs began to fail. By the second week, every organ in his body was failing. As per his wishes, we tried everything to try to resuscitate him when his heart finally gave in, but to no avail.

Mr. Kensington died exactly three weeks after he came into the hospital.

Every day of those three weeks, we attempted to find some family or friends that he may have had, but we were unable to do so except for a friend from his company whom Mr. Kensington had given us the number of "should things get quite bad."

"I am afraid that unfortunately I don't know Mr. Kensington too much outside of work, but of course if there is no one else, I will make arrangements for his funeral," the voice on the other end of the phone quietly stated.

Over the course of the COVID-19 pandemic, my colleagues and I encountered many like Mr. Kensington. It is heartbreaking whenever someone dies alone.

Before a person dies, they see who their true friends are. Many experience shock and depression when faced with the harsh reality that those who they thought were their friends were just work colleagues or acquaintances.

A reemerging theme I have noticed with patients at death's door is a sudden clarity on priorities. Mr. Kensington pleaded with me on how he felt "so foolish" that he had valued career over social and family connections. This is an incredibly common sorrow that health-care workers observed in the vast amount of death during the pandemic. Patients spoke of bitterness at work taking so much of their *time*, particularly when *time* was something they no longer had. They expressed heartbreak at prioritizing work, career, money, etc. over friends and family.

When patients are at death's doorstep, I have found that those who are ready are rarely alone. And those with immense regret almost always are.

Thus, it seems, a life of fulfillment and without regret is one with *others*. Having loved ones, which oftentimes come in the form of family or very close and deep friendships, can give meaning to life. This notion is supported in research done in the field of psychology and sociology. Decades of academic research on happiness has consistently highlighted the strong association of positive friendship experiences with individual happiness. The friendship-happiness link has been observed across age, ethnic, and cultural groups.[13]

In a landmark study, researchers compared the upper 10 percent of consistently very happy people with average and very unhappy people. The very happy people were highly social and had stronger romantic and other social relationships than less happy groups.[14]

Conversely, studies have shown that loneliness has a negative effect on people's health and happiness. Our brains and bodies are designed to exist in the context of friendships and meaningful relationships. Our ancestors relied on living in small, close-knit tribes to survive in the harsh wilderness. Having close friendships during such an era was literally the difference between life and death. Those who lived in isolation did not survive to raise another generation. These evolutionary forces have formatted our very brains with neural circuits requiring meaningful relationships to achieve health and happiness.[15] These circuits interact with every part of our body, influencing our blood vessels, nervous system, and heart. And so, our physiology evolved in the context of friendships.

This is why for me, as a doctor, meaningful relationships are not just critical for my patients' happiness, although of course this alone is an incredibly important reason. But rather, the absence of friendships can result in devastating health consequences.

A well-known study in the UK found that loneliness was associated with a 29 percent increase in risk of heart disease and a 32 percent increase in risk of stroke.[16] Higher systolic blood pressure, body mass index, and higher cholesterol have all been associated with loneliness as well. Loneliness increases the likelihood of early death by 26 percent, which is roughly equivalent to smoking fifteen cigarettes a day or having obesity.[17] It seems like I should be writing prescriptions for "friendship" for my patients, as evidently, it'd be just as efficacious as most medications!

Being lonely is quite literally killing us. Our bodies and brains have evolved to thrive on meaningful social connection. But the world we live in would be unrecognizable to the tribe-dwelling cavemen our neural circuitry has evolved from and does not facilitate these social needs. With the internet, we are more connected than at any other time in human history. Our brains are saturated with an influx of notifications from social media, but some research suggests that we are starving for *meaningful relationships*.[18] As a result, our modern society is faced with an unprecedented epidemic of loneliness, and the data suggests that this is a public health crisis.[19]

Doctors and nurses try hard to be there for patients, especially during the final chapter of their lives when they pass away. Nobody deserves to die alone, and health-care providers, especially nurses, try to provide comfort to patients as they die. The onus of providing companionship at death is something that has caused a large toll on the mental and emotional well-being of health-care workers during the COVID-19 surges.

Nurses particularly were at the forefront of the pandemic. During the surges, when faced with incredible amounts of patient death, they would often be the sole comforters for patients who were alone. Studies indicate that this had a significant impact on the mental health of nurses, as they were found to have higher anxiety and depression than the general population and a higher risk for PTSD than recent veterans or patients after traumatic injury.[20]

Anecdotally, I recall during the Omicron surge when we saw many heartbreaking cases of patients dying alone and full of regret; the obligation of being there for them in their final moments weighed heavily on the hearts of my nurse colleagues. But this burden enacted a tax on their own emotional well-being. The desolation of those dying alone is not dissipated but rather is converted to the heartache of those doing the comforting. Day by day, attempting to fill the vast empty void chipped away at our own emotional fortitude.

This dilemma was identified by administrative committees in hospitals all over the country during the peak of the pandemic. At our institution, we all tried to implement mindfulness practices to curb the burnout, but it was incredibly difficult to practically implement.

Despite my best efforts, after being faced with the immense death during the pandemic, I still do not have a good response to comfort patients when they are faced with loneliness in death. I find that I default to vaguely comforting them and holding their hand. We health-care workers try our best, though no amount of assuaging can truly fill the void. But my experience has caused me to invest more in my own family and friendships so that when I die, I will have the comfort of those around me who have given my life meaning.

Human beings are social creatures. Meaningful relationships with friends and family are crucial ingredients to a purposeful life. We do not know when death will come for us. Investing in these relationships to give our lives meaning should be a priority so we do not regret missing out on this pivotal aspect of life when it is too late.

Chapter 3

Always attempt.

Winter in Chicago is bleak by anyone's standards. The frigid air freezes the inside of your nose as you breathe in, and the gusts of wind cut through to your very bones. Although the weather in March is not as bitter as the frigid tundra that is Chicago in December through February, in my experience living in Chicago, there is something rather worse about March. With March in Chicago, you don't know what you're going to get. Outside your door could await either an icy, crisp wind with temperatures in the twenties—or a (relatively) pleasant day with temperatures in the fifties. While the rest of the country seems to be celebrating the arrival of spring, you have to put on three layers before stepping outside.

The frosty weather never bothered Chicago native Bart Scully, however. The biting chill only pushed the sixty-seven-year-old to run harder. He put on his running shoes and windbreaker one brisk Chicago March morning, and he stepped foot outside into the bitter cold. His jogging route took him alongside the lakefront where he greeted the sunrise, golden rays reflecting off the surface of Lake Michigan to pierce through the arctic air. He dashed through the lakefront trail, turning onto the riverwalk. Ordinarily bustling with tourists and families, the Chicago Riverwalk was quiet and peaceful with businesses still setting up shop and cruises getting ready to set sail.

After the riverwalk, Bart liked to run down Michigan Avenue while it was still serene in the early mornings to see the rising sun break through between the towering skyscrapers. But this morning, he decided to cut his jog short. Bart wasn't sure what it was, but he felt that something was off in his body. His muscles were already tired and sore, as if he had been exercising for hours.

Bart Scully first noticed that he was having trouble catching his breath after coming home from his daily jog. He started feeling scratchiness in his throat and, later in the day, began having a dry cough. He turned on the TV and began flipping through the channels. He thought: *Maybe if I just relax and take it easy, I'll feel better soon.* Eventually, he landed on the news where the news anchor noted COVID had now spread to all fifty states.

Unfortunately, he did not feel better after a day of rest. He came into the hospital after he began experiencing fevers alongside shortness of breath, expecting to be told it was just a viral illness (one of the "normal ones," not COVID) and to go home and rest.

"I haven't really been keeping up with the news, but I figure it's probably nothing too serious. My daughter insisted that I come in to get it checked out. She keeps up with these things," he said when I came in.

His COVID test was positive.

It was a time of tension and anxiety in the hospital. COVID was rapidly spreading across the country, and everyone was waiting on edge for the inevitable wave that would stress test the US health-care system. The hospital had erected a large tent with temporary rooms in anticipation of being overrun by COVID cases. All elective surgeries and visits had been indefinitely postponed. We were preparing for war, and uneasiness was in the air as we dreaded the oncoming onslaught.

With the increasing amounts of COVID patients coming into the emergency rooms and urgent cares, the supply of PPE was already dwindling. Hospitals across the nation issued guidelines on how to reuse PPE, such as N95 masks. All the while, a significant portion of the population was ignoring social distancing guidelines that were critical to curb the surges in cases.

Furthermore, as providers, we did not know as much about COVID as we do now. We were navigating uncharted territory, fighting an enemy before acquiring the proper intel. It was difficult to tell patients what to expect in terms of their illness severity as we were still learning ourselves. This was further complicated by mixed messaging from both government officials and media that downplayed COVID-19, or worse, painted doctors as scapegoats. This uncertainty put both providers and patients on edge.

When we told Bart Scully the news about his COVID test, he asked the questions most patients had when they were found to have COVID during that era: *What does this mean? How did I get this? How long will I need to be in the hospital? Am I going to live?* We tried our best to answer with the little information we had about COVID at the time, while also trying to instill hope. We explained that we would closely watch him for a couple days in the hospital. If he did well, then we would discharge him home to complete his quarantine.

Mr. Scully had a chronic metabolic disease, and we discussed how the emerging data on COVID indicated that he would be at increased risk for severe disease, but we reassured him that we'd keep a close eye on him and take appropriate action should we feel he was headed that way.

When I came by later in the day to check in on him, he was typing furiously on his laptop. He was deep in concentration, and his fingers appeared to be a blur as his words filled up the screen.

I asked him what he was typing. He described that he was an author and pointed to the sticker on the back of his laptop that said "always be writing" and grinned.

"That's my motto!" he bellowed enthusiastically. "Writing can be a difficult undertaking, but I've found that if I write every day, I'll be able to get where I need to be over time."

Over the course of the night, his difficulty breathing increased, and his oxygen levels declined. Each time I checked on him, he was more breathless and his voice was raspier. I spoke with him again, and we discussed that he may need to be intubated if his current trajectory continued. He understood.

"I'm very proud of my accomplishments in life." He gestured to his laptop on which he would furiously type his manuscripts. "If my life is at its end, so be it. I have spent my life doing what I love and do not have qualms. I always tried so that I would never have to wonder *what if*. But I think I have a few more pages in me, and I'd like you to do everything you can to help me survive to get those out if possible."

I nodded.

The conversation turned to his previous books. He described that when he was in grad school studying literature, he'd had a severe writer's block. For months, he would try outlining, brainstorming ideas, discussing with fellow writers, but could not figure out an idea worth writing.

A veteran writer gave him advice that he said changed his life. "Just write *something*. Whatever comes to your mind. Keep attempting. No more planning or preparation. Just write."

He began writing. The first few pages were a haphazard collection of thoughts with no direction. He spent years writing manuscripts that were rejected by publishers.

"That's all part of the process. If you want to grow in anything, you're going to have to falter before you fly," he told me. "My mentor told me that I have to always be kind to myself. If I view my own work too harshly, I'll become discouraged and lose motivation."

But then something clicked, and over the next six months, he wrote a manuscript that would become his first published book.

Mr. Scully told me that he had diligently stuck to this advice over his writing career of twenty-five years. And because of this, he had published nine books during this time frame.

"I tell everyone this advice. I don't care if you're a photographer, writer, artist, or scientist. Keep attempting. Not planning on an attempt. Not preparing for an attempt. *Attempting*."

This is hardly a novel mindset. Afterall, in the eighteenth century, French philosopher Voltaire noted that "perfect is the enemy of good."

As I get to know patients in the final chapter of their lives, many express regret that they did not try to pursue their passion. A common theme that emerges is a sense of perfectionism that impedes the initiation. Fear of not getting everything right the first time results in a paralysis of even beginning the process.

Interestingly, there is ongoing research on how this form of "perfectionism" may actually be detrimental to health, as some studies show that life expectancy for perfectionists is reduced by 51 percent.[21] Perhaps "perfectionism" should have a surgeon general's warning!

It is a quality I have observed consistently in the productive patients I have met, regardless of their field. Variations of "Just start *doing*. Get your reps in, and don't be afraid of failure."

During the final chapter of their lives, many patients have remorse that they did not pursue certain passions of theirs, such as writing plays, learning languages, etc. Often, they were waiting for certain inspiration to strike or to achieve mastery of a specific skill before trying to pursue their dream. They may have even spent a significant portion of their lives engaging in things to *prepare* or *plan*, anything but actually *doing*.

For example, early on during the COVID pandemic, I met two separate patients, both of whom were middle-aged men who bemoaned not trying their hand at stand-up comedy. They had taken online courses designed to help and even read books, but they never got around to actually being on the mic at a comedy club. Regrettably, one of these individuals passed away, but the other man recovered well after COVID.

As the pandemic improved, and businesses began reopening, the surviving patient signed up for open mic night at the Comedy Store and sent me a picture of him doing a set with the note that he couldn't believe he had never simply tried *doing* before and felt lucky his brush with death had given him this perspective. He noted that he bombed, but he had a couple jokes that worked and was already signed up for another open mic later in the week to keep building on that experience.

Patients on their deathbeds reveal many regrets that could have been remedied by simply *doing*. Waiting too long to ask someone out or to ask a significant other for marriage (or some other progression of a relationship) until it is too late. Not telling an individual they love them. You'd be surprised how common it is for patients at their deathbed to regret not initiating or investing more into their relationship with their significant others. This is a regret experienced by both the patients and their loved ones.

Another common regret is constantly preparing to start a business and then never actually executing on the idea. Of course, hindsight is 20/20, and we're all geniuses in our minds; I've had at least five patients tell me they had thought of the smart doorbell but had been too afraid to take the risk to try making it.

At least three patients shared with me that they had an idea for the next Great American Novel, and another four told me they had been meaning to work on a screenplay but were too afraid they weren't good writers to even try. Frankly, after hearing them describe their ideas, they all seem like fascinating stories that should have been told.

That is not to say that any of these individuals would have been successful in their endeavors if they had tried. But I doubt they would have regretted trying. I've cared for many fulfilled patients who found meaning in trying, even if their projects did not result in "success" (traditionally defined by marketplace response).

It is commonplace for nurses or doctors to listen to patients lament on their deathbeds about *what could have been*. We heard a lot of *what ifs* during the pandemic surges when times were bleak. We never heard anyone disappointed in trying something and it not turning out as well as they'd hoped.

Cutting edge psychological science supports this notion. Fearing failure or punishing oneself for failing causes paralysis, as one will not continue to attempt. Researchers have found that a critical trait in resiliency to accomplish great things is self-compassion. Self-compassion, through self-kindness, connection, and mindfulness, may allow individuals to strive for mastery and goal accomplishment, while also holding these goals lightly and demonstrating resilience when adversity arises.[22] Later in this book, we will meet Samia Khan who will teach us the power of being kind to ourselves through self-compassion.

The advice Mr. Scully's mentor imparted upon him was conscious of a need for self-compassion. He was told to be kind to himself and frame the rejection by agents and publishers as simply part of the process. Bart Scully practiced self-compassion when going through writer's block as well as when he experienced rejection, and kept trying, which eventually resulted in his first published book.

I have found that fulfilled patients take risks and *just try*. They do not punish themselves for their failures. And they treat themselves with compassion whenever they stumble. They know that falling down and getting back up is all part of the growth needed to accomplish anything.

Over the next day, Bart Scully's breathing improved. He was released from the hospital later in the week.

He sent me a card a month later stating that the writing he did while in the hospital had sparked an idea for another book that he was in the process of writing. He had trashed the draft he'd written in the hospital, but attempting that one had inspired him to write another book, which he had pitched to his publisher. He wrote that he'd send me a copy once it got published.

Ten books; infinite attempts.

Chapter 4

Live surrounded by gratitude.

Nowadays, mention of Ukraine evokes images of brave Ukrainians coming together to protect their homeland against a larger hostile force. Invading armies have made an entire generation of Ukrainians vulnerable to the horrors of war as they see their families broken, economies collapsed, and communities ravaged. Almost overnight, lives of peace were replaced by unrelenting bloodshed. This is not the Ukraine that Vira Boiko fondly shared her childhood memories of.

Vira Boiko immigrated from Ukraine to the United States when she was in her early thirties. She came from a quiet, peaceful village "where everyone knew each other and every mother was a mother to every child in the town." She loved growing up there and was sad to go when her husband needed to move to the US for work. She moved to the Midwest with her husband and infant son in order to find a new life for her family and found employment as a house cleaner. She had been living in this country for the past thirty years and boasted, "We've created a lovely little life for ourselves where we have everything we could want."

When the pandemic hit, she could not work as she normally had. In the first few months of the pandemic, she had socially distanced as recommended by public health officials.

"Not everyone in our town did, but my husband and I followed the guidelines so that we could protect the elderly in our community."

However, soon she realized she would need to go back to work in order to pay her expenses.

"It's easy for some to social distance when they can work from home or social distance at work. But it is not easy for many who need to go to work and rely on our paychecks," she explained. She returned to cleaning homes for her clients.

After a couple months of working, she started coughing up thick phlegm and was short of breath when she'd try to walk. She was afraid it might be COVID, so she came into the Emergency Department (ED) to get tested.

In the ED, she was found to have both COVID and bacterial pneumonia. The ED team decided to page us to admit her to the hospital to give her some oxygen support as well as give her IV antibiotics for the pneumonia.

As I entered her room, she greeted me with an enthusiastic wave. She wore a bright orange cardigan sweater and yellow pants. On her neck was a necklace with a silver, nine-pointed star pendant, appearing a brilliant gold as it reflected the shining light. Yet somehow the energy emanating from her face was even brighter than her clothes.

"Thank you so much Dr. Abbasi!" she said earnestly after I explained the plan.

As I exited the room, I felt quite warm from the gratitude.

When I saw her the next morning on the wards, she was looking at the sunrise through the window and journaling in a black moleskin notebook, the frenetic scratching of the fountain pen against the paper interrupted every few seconds as she pondered her next thought. The golden sunrise reflected off the nine-pointed star pendant.

She looked up and smiled, setting aside the notebook on the side table. I asked her if she would feel comfortable telling me what she was writing about.

"Yes, of course. So the backstory is ..." she paused for a second before continuing. I could tell she was calculating whether to share something before proceeding. "Fifteen years ago, I was ... assaulted by someone who I considered a friend."

As soon as she finished her sentence, the tension in the room became palpable. The room felt like it had chilled twenty degrees in a second as I had not realized that the conversation would take such a serious tone. But when I looked at her, she gave me a reassuring smile. I gently asked if she was sure that she was comfortable and wanted to share.

"Of course, yes. I'm glad you asked, because this is something I am quite passionate about," she said.

With her warmth, the chill left as quickly as it had come.

"To help me recover my mental health, my best friend took me to the Baha'i temple an hour away, where I learned to connect to a higher power and engage in mindfulness activities."

Many years ago, I had visited the very temple she spoke of when I was touring architectural marvels on the National Register of Historic Places. I was mesmerized by the stunning white dome structure surrounded by luscious gardens and dazzling fountains. Intricate calligraphy is carved into the columns, and at the top of each column is a nine-pointed star.

"The spiritual assembly there encouraged us to engage in gratitude exercises. Every day I write what I'm grateful for or an occasion where someone expressed gratitude to me. It started as a simple daily exercise that I was not sure I'd continue long term. However, I noticed that my whole mental state changed. I began feeling happier without having to try. My life felt more meaningful."

Compellingly, Vira Boiko is not the only patient I have met who engaged in active gratitude. Some journal about gratitude like Mrs. Boiko. Others will incorporate themes of gratitude in their mindfulness or prayer.

When I think about gratitude as a physician, it is not some vague concept or feel-good message. Gratitude has distinct physiologic pathways and consequential effects on the human body that neuroscientists have been able to identify.

Gratitude manifests itself as increased activity in the areas of the brain known as the anterior cingulate cortex and medial prefrontal cortex.[23] This is quite significant as the medial prefrontal cortex is the component in the brain that sets the whole context for our life. Neuroscientist Dr. Andrew Huberman notes that the medial prefrontal cortex is what can take a life experience and make it a positive experience that results in positive health benefits, or a negative experience that can negatively affect your health.[24] Incorporating practices of gratitude in your life trains your brain to encode your life experience in a positive manner.

Psychologists researching the significance of gratitude in our lives have shown that gratitude has been associated with an increased sense of personal satisfaction.[25] It has been scientifically shown to make you a better friend.[26] It has been concluded to be important to psychological well-being.[27] Daily gratitude was even shown to be uniquely critical for daily well-being for combat veterans suffering from PTSD.[28]

As a physician, what really makes me excited is a recent groundbreaking study where researchers studied how the practice of incorporating gratitude affected physiologic mediators related to metabolic and cardiovascular diseases. Gratitude has been shown to be linked with certain changes in your actual physical state, such as decreasing your heart rate.[29] They found that having a gratitude practice resulted in reductions in amygdala reactivity following the gratitude task. The amygdala is the part of your brain associated with fear and strong negative emotions.

Importantly, gratitude was also associated with reductions in the stimulated production of TNF-*a* and IL-6.[30] These are proinflammatory cytokines that have been shown to be contributors to a host of cardiovascular diseases,[31] metabolic diseases such as diabetes,[32] and even some cancers.[33] Thus, this emerging scientific data demonstrated how a gratitude-oriented mindset prevents cardiovascular disease, metabolic disease, and some cancers through specific biologic pathways. Physiologically, gratitude has a similar significance to one's health as regular exercise and eating healthy!

Vira Boiko described to me that since she had begun practicing active gratitude several times a week, she noticed that those around her began feeling more positive, and they in turn would express gratitude to her. It became a vicious cycle of positivity.

"I never knew that such a simple task that takes me a few minutes each week could have such a profound impact on both my life and those around me. I used to hesitate so much when expressing gratitude. Sure, I'd say 'thank you' and was polite, but expressing specific, sincere gratitude to those around me for all they've done to make my life wonderful was something I had always hesitated to do before."

The science suggests that most people hesitate to express gratitude, just like Mrs. Boiko used to do. When considering whether to express gratitude to a fellow human being, we consistently significantly underestimate how surprised recipients will be about why we were grateful, overestimate how awkward recipients will feel, and significantly underestimate how positive recipients will feel.[34] We have the power to completely change the neurology of others in a positive manner, but we underestimate the impact we could have on those around us.

Knowing that others are intentionally grateful or supporting us changes the way our bodies actually process stimuli. There is a fascinating experiment in which college students were exposed to painful stimuli. In the experiment, they had a partner who either intentionally or unintentionally bore part of their pain. The catch is that the students knew whether their partner was intentionally or unintentionally sharing in their pain. Afterward, the students had to rate their perceived pain intensity. Pain was perceived as less intense when receiving help was interpreted as intentional, relative to unintentional.[35]

We have the power to literally take pain away from those around us through intentional support and positively interacting with others.

Vira Boiko's breathing declined over the next few days. Her oxygen support was increased to the maximum level of high-flow nasal cannula, and even on that, her oxygen levels were borderline. We continued aggressive therapies to treat the COVID and pneumonia, but it seemed like her condition was worsening every day.

We discussed that she would need to be intubated to give her lungs some rest and allow her body to get adequate oxygenation and fight the infection. I explained to her that although we would continue to try our best, she was in a very critical condition.

While gulping for air, she slowly said, "Thank you, Dr. Abbasi. If it is my time to leave this world, I am okay with that. I am grateful for a gratifying life with warm people. But I hope this is not the last time I see you."

That would be the last thing she said to me. She was on the ventilator for two weeks, but one day, her heart stopped beating and went into a fatal arrhythmia. We did CPR for forty-five minutes but were unable to bring her back.

I called time of death and went to the nurses station to call her husband.

Meeting Vira Boiko led me to research the role of gratitude in healthy living. With the previously discussed findings, I have begun to instill her practice of engaging in active gratitude at least twice a week.

Perhaps even more importantly, I have become far more generous in expressing my gratitude to others. In turn, I have noticed that others have begun to do the same to me. I find that as we share gratitude with each other, we illuminate each other's lives. In the dark days of the pandemic, everything felt a little bit brighter when we were able to express gratitude to each other.

Chapter 5

Instill daily habits for compounding growth.

Your body is in a state of harmony between decay and growth. A delicate balance of yin and yang exists as certain processes are working to build up your body while others are working to break your body down. This diverse array of mechanisms exists in a fragile state of equilibrium, each intricately functioning in relation to another like gears of a finely tuned watch. This stability is important to maintain our bodies in a healthy state. When the scale tips toward either end, the balance turns into a state of disarray and disease occurs.

Grappling with this state of disarray was a battle Mary Roger is all too familiar with. At age fifty-two, Mary Roger is extremely young (by hospital standards), but she has had quite a difficult life thus far.

She was born with a very rare genetic disease called alpha-1 antitrypsin deficiency. Alpha-1 antitrypsin is an important protein that protects the airways and lungs from damage. It is an important balance against another naturally occurring family of proteins called "proteolytic enzymes," which can break down the lung without an inhibitor. Patients with alpha-1 antitrypsin deficiency are born without the inhibitor and thus the protection conferred by this important check on the proteolytic enzymes. The delicate balance is tipped in favor of breaking down.

Mary has a severe variant of the disease that affects both her lungs and her liver. Because of this disease, she has needed to regularly see several specialists including pulmonology (lungs) and gastroenterology (liver and bowels) doctors ever since she was a baby. She is quite diligent with her health care, always following up regularly and never missing an appointment or lab test.

Her dangerous chronic disease made it particularly scary when she learned she had COVID.

It started as just a fever, as it did for many patients. But within a day, she had such profound difficulty breathing that she had to come into the hospital. Her pulmonologist had astutely advised her to come to the emergency room if she ever felt any respiratory symptoms because of the very high risk of a severe lung infection. Upon arriving, she was quickly admitted to the hospital and started on oxygen support.

Mary told me that as she has learned to live with her health condition, she had worked to instill healthy habits to give her the best chance at living a normal life. Interestingly, she would always mention how her disease had instilled her with discipline that had given her "a new life."

This discipline began as incorporating healthy habits into her daily life as suggested by her doctor. She began going to the gym four times a week and made sure that she did cardiovascular exercise every day to keep her lungs and heart healthy. For the first three months, she did not notice any differences besides a general "feeling better." But over time, she noted that her breathing would be much easier, especially when exercising. Her muscles became stronger. Most significantly, her regular coughing fits had almost entirely stopped. She noted that a small habit, such as regularly going to the gym, made almost no difference on a daily level, but it compounded over time to make significant changes.

She began using this compounding philosophy in other parts of her life. After reading a biography of Warren Buffet in her junior year of college, she began investing regularly into an S&P 500 index fund. She started with small amounts in college, and once she had a job, she made it a goal to invest 10 percent of her income every month. She equated it to doing a "rep at the gym," as allocating 10 percent made almost no difference to her lifestyle, and her monthly contributions did not make a big difference to her brokerage. However, after a decade of doing this, her contributions had compounded (both due to her regular contributions, but more importantly due to the 8 percent annualized compounding growth of the stock market) to the point that she was able to buy her first home with cash at the age of thirty-five! (This may or may not be practical anymore depending on the state of the real estate market at time of reading.)

Mary took this philosophy of regular habits compounding over time to her relationships as well. She was disappointed that she was not as close to her younger sister ever since she moved to the other coast. Rather than let their relationship wither away, Mary decided to do something about it. Mary developed habits of regularly checking up on her sister every day via a phone call or even text. Regardless of how short the conversation was (even if it was one quick text that said "Hi!") she made it a habit that she could not go on with her day without checking in with her sister—just like going to the gym. Although it did not make a noticeable difference in the short term, she noticed that it had slowly resulted in her sister being much closer to her over time.

After six months, she noted that almost half of the time, her sister would reach out to her first before she even got to. After about a year, they began planning to go on a vacation together. After two years, her sister named her godmother of her first child.

Over the course of her second day at the hospital, Mary's breathing worsened. She was on the maximum oxygen supports on high-flow nasal cannula, one of the highest support we can provide with breathing besides intubation. We transferred her to the ICU to keep a close eye on her.

At this time, I explained to Mary that due to her severe chronic disease, it was very likely she would need to be intubated as the COVID progressed.

During the era of COVID, it had become standard practice to discuss a patient's preference regarding whether they would like to be intubated whenever they are admitted to the hospital, known as clarifying their "code status." This was done to ensure that there was no confusion as to the patient's preference, should their respiratory status deteriorate.

Addressing code status when admitting a patient needs to be done tactfully, as you don't want to scare the patient by talking about intubation when they're currently requiring very minimal oxygen support. But you also want to be clear about helping them make an informed decision. COVID-19 can have a rapid course as a disease, and you never know how quickly or severely it will progress in a patient.

I gently explained to her that due to her severe lung disease, she would likely need to be intubated. Furthermore, the chance of her surviving to eventually be extubated was low.

"I understand." Mary spoke softly. "Ever since being diagnosed with this disease, I've known that I could die from a lung infection. I have worked hard to take care of my body to always give myself the best life I can. But I have always known death. I go to support groups with people with the same disease as me. Many of my friends from that group have since passed away, many of them over the past year with COVID."

Mary smiled and looked me in the eye. Her eyes filled with tears, but none rolled down her cheek.

"I have always lived my life so that I am ready."

I was reminded of Captain Greg and nodded.

When I went to her room the next morning for my next shift, she had been intubated. The breathing tube in her mouth delivering gusts of breath and the regular beating of her heart monitor indicated that even in this critically ill state, her body was fighting.

Against all odds, over the next three days, her body kept up the fight and her lungs eventually began clearing toward the end of the third day. Her entire team was surprised at her progress, as most of our COVID patients with this severe chronic lung disease have far greater difficulty fighting the virus.

The neurologic and respiratory status of patients intubated in the ICU is very carefully monitored. A delicate equilibrium is maintained to ensure the patient has adequate pain control and sedation so they are comfortable and their body can heal, while also making sure they are not overly sedated, which can hinder recovery. This is achieved through a painstakingly detailed titration of "drips" (what we call continuous IV medications) alongside detailed observations of the patients. The patient is examined, and the results are used to calculate their level of sedation using an algorithm. The "RASS scoring system" is one of the most commonly used scales to determine the appropriate sedation level. This score helps practitioners to adjust the rate of the drips.

For these patients intubated in the ICU, we typically do a daily "spontaneous breathing trial" during which we carefully turn down the settings of the ventilator to see how their breathing is with minimal support. During this time, we also temporarily reduce the sedation drips to allow them to be more awake, while still making sure they are comfortable and pain free. This allows us to see how the patient is progressing in terms of their respiratory status. It also allows the patient's lungs to do a daily exercise to increase the strength of the muscles that facilitate breathing. Having our patients do this exercise allows them to recover quicker and even be extubated earlier.[36]

On the first day of being on the ventilator, Mary struggled with the spontaneous breathing trial. Her breathing muscles strained to pull in air, and she was not able to breathe without support for more than a few minutes. By the end of the week, Mary was able to breath independently during her entire daily spontaneous breathing trial of two hours, and she was able to be extubated.

We discussed Mary that week during Grand Rounds, a hospital-wide conference during which a physician shares an important case from which the other doctors at the hospital can discuss and learn. All of the lung and critical care specialists in attendance agreed that it was Mary's daily healthy habits and regular cardiovascular exercise that had saved her life. "A true testament to the compounding nature of daily habits!" one of the ICU doctors exclaimed in awe.

Her small daily habits had strengthened her lungs over time to the point that she was able to overcome the slim odds afforded to her by her genetics and fight off a dangerous respiratory virus.

Mary is an extraordinary example of the cumulative effect of daily actions, but small, regular acts resulting in phenomenal accomplishments is something we've seen in many fulfilled individuals during the final chapter of their lives. Over the course of the pandemic, I've had the honor of meeting a painter who began by simply allocating a few minutes a day, a writer who wrote a *New York Times* bestseller by writing a paragraph a day, and an accomplished orchestra musician who began by taking a half hour after work to practice their instrument.

I have a patient I see in my clinic who had been suffering with pain from arthritis for years. No amount of over-the-counter pain medication ever made a significant dent. Last year, she had tried a course of physical therapy for a couple weeks, but did not feel it helped much then and stopped. She wasn't ready to proceed with surgery for a full knee replacement yet however. We discussed that we would try to see if we could alleviate her symptoms through physical therapy before considering orthopedic surgery. She began incorporating the exercises recommended by her physical therapist into her daily schedule. She did not notice any changes in the first few weeks or even months, but she kept at it. Half a year later, she noticed that the pain was now almost nonexistent. Changing and strengthening our bodies and minds requires regular, persistent work over time.

However, I've also met some with regret at the end of their life who were too afraid to start upon this journey due to the daunting size of the task. I have met individuals who wished they had learned that instrument, worked on their relationships, or created that website. But out of fear of the size of the task, they never took the first step. I have found that patients who are able to achieve big tasks will typically break them up into very small "biteable" chunks, and use that to incorporate small actions into their daily lives.

The cumulative effect of daily actions is evident (and in many cases, far more obvious) when observing patients with negative habits. For example, extreme obesity and high cholesterol are both drastic states that manifest from daily habits of an unhealthy diet (although research has suggested that there is also a strong genetic contribution to both of the above). Dental cavities are the result of lack of dental hygiene, such as brushing or flossing. Joint and muscle issues often stem from a sedentary lifestyle.

Health outcomes from blatant negative physical habits such as smoking or eating fast food daily are rather obvious. I have noted that the effect of certain ambiguous daily habits on one's mental health is more subtle to identify in patients, but has an equally negative effect on their health.

For instance, I have had several patients who have noted that daily consumption of social media has resulted in exacerbation of depression or anxiety over time. For some individuals, habitual persistent use of these social media sites rewires the way our brains process and frame social well-being. Anecdotally, many of these patients have noted improvements in their health when decreasing this daily habit. The research on this topic is ongoing, although some studies have found that social media is associated with various mental health issues, such as depression.[37]

Our days consist of habits that occur almost automatically every day. Like singular steps on the journey of life, certain habits help us build toward what our goals are, while others may take us off the path without us even realizing. Patients who express that they've lived a meaningful life have consistently identified what their daily habits are and analyzed whether they are consistent with their overall life goals. They know that there is power in seemingly insignificant actions when they are done regularly over time, both for and against you. They know that great things can be accomplished when broken up in small chunks to be done every day.

Thirty minutes after the breathing tube was removed, Mary asked how many more days she had to stay in the hospital.

"I have to exercise! But first, am I allowed to use my phone here? I have to call my sister."

Chapter 6

Marry your best friend.

If the world were ending around you, what would you do? In the year 79 CE, the inhabitants of the great city of Pompeii faced this very question, and due to a quirk of geological phenomenon, their answers have been preserved for perpetuity. The prosperous ancient Roman city, established since the times of the Ancient Greeks, was wiped out in a moment when the volcano Mount Vesuvius erupted.

The merciless eruption destroyed the entire city. Many of the men, women, and children living their lives in the vibrant city were dead instantly due to the heat wave from the eruption, in which temperatures exceeded over 500 degrees Fahrenheit. This was followed by a thick layer of ash coating everything and everyone. This ash calcified, freezing the devastated city in time and preserving all of its inhabitants in the exact state they were in at death.[38]

Many ran in panic in a futile attempt to avoid their inevitable fate. Others hid in their homes before being buried in the rubble. Some begged for mercy from their gods, thinking the calamity befalling them to surely be the end of the world.

Among this chaos, two individuals decided that the last emotion they wanted to experience was not the fear and horror surrounding them, but rather love and comfort. They held each other in their arms and comforted each other. One of them rested their head on the other's chest the moment Mount Vesuvius took their lives and preserved their love in an eternal embrace still visible at the Pompeii archaeological site.

When doctors on the internal medicine service get paged by the emergency room doctors to admit a patient, we typically receive a room number with a name and quick medical summary. So when I first received the page with one room number, 605-A/B, and two names, I did a double take. *Must be a typo*, I thought.

As I entered the room, Maria and José Sanchez were sitting together, holding each other's hands. Maria was resting her head on José's shoulder, and their arms were wrapped around each other, making it tough to see at first glance where one stopped and the other started. They had both done everything right during the first few months of the pandemic, taking extra precautions due to their ages, as they were both in their eighties. They had limited their in-person social interactions with close family only, used grocery delivery apps so that they wouldn't have to go outside unnecessarily, and always wore masks when they did go outside.

After a few months, they couldn't bear not seeing their grandchildren and decided to have them visit as long as they in turn were careful who they visited. But unfortunately, five days later, Mr. Sanchez began having fevers and difficulty breathing when walking. The next day, Mrs. Sanchez began experiencing the same symptoms, and they both decided to come to the emergency room, where they were found to have COVID.

This was during a time when, due to the surge in COVID cases, the hospital was at over a 100 percent capacity. Rather than hospitalize Mr. and Mrs. Sanchez in different rooms, the hospital staff opted to simply add another hospital bed to one of the rooms so they could be together, much to the delight of Maria and José.

"Oh, I couldn't bear the thought of spending a night apart!" Maria sighed. José nodded his head in agreement.

Mr. and Mrs. Sanchez would tell me cute stories from their lives every time I would visit their room. Their meet-cute was right out of a storybook. They grew up together, and as kids, they were inseparable, hanging out every day, biking to the bench by the creek to meet at "our spot" as José would describe it.

When they started high school, José began developing feelings for Maria. But he did not dare express them to her out of fear of jeopardizing their friendship. The feelings did not go away but only grew the longer they spent time together. Still, sharing his feelings with her would be no small feat. *What if she does not think of me that way and I lose my closest friend?* he could not stop asking himself. Alas, the power of his feelings eventually overcame his doubts. It took him a whole year to build up the courage to finally confess his feelings to her in sophomore year.

"What took you so long? Yes, of course I like you!" Maria recalls responding before kissing him.

Their love continued to grow in high school, and in senior year, they were relieved when they both opened their Cornell acceptance letters.

José majored in computer science, and Maria majored in sociology. After graduation, they moved to the San Francisco Bay area to start their lives.

A year later, they visited their hometown of Burlington, Vermont. When they were walking by the creek ("our spot!" Maria interjected into the story), bright flowers and shimmering lights adorned the side of the path. A picnic was set up with Maria's favorite wine and an assortment of cheeses. José knelt down on one knee and proposed.

Over the next decade, they would have three children. After retiring, they moved back to their hometown and bought a small house near the creek.

"We've had a very happy life. We're each other's best friends. He is my everything, and I am his."

Over the next few days, both José's and Maria's breathing became more labored. They slowly began requiring higher levels of oxygen, with their progression matching each other's.

From the very first day, both Maria and José were adamant that they did not want to be intubated should their breathing require it, or have aggressive measures done should they pass away.

We worked diligently to try to improve their breathing. By now, the whole ward had become invested in their love story. We tried every medical intervention we could think of to maximize their changes, but despite our best efforts, the virus kept progressing and taking away their breathing.

By the next day, it became clear that they both would likely succumb to the infection. I called their children, whom I had gotten to know well over the phone, and told them they should fly over as soon as possible.

That night, I received the page at 1:05 a.m. reading room number 605-A. *José's room!* I started running over.

Has Maria realized? I thought.

Twenty seconds later, as I was still running over to the room, I got another page reading room number 605-B. *Maria's room!*

I entered the room and saw Maria and José together in the same bed, still holding each other. Neither of them was breathing, but I thought I saw faint smiles on their lips. Maria's head rested on José's chest. *Just like the lovers of Pompeii,* I thought.

As a physician, you see many couples. Some just recently started their relationships and others who have been together for decades. When one's partner is hospitalized, it can be a traumatic stress test for the relationship.

This was especially true during the COVID pandemic surges, as seeing the dramatic progression of the disease in one's loved ones such that they are at death's door within days is a truly ghastly experience. Unfortunately, the stress of the experience can be enough to break some already fragile relationships. However, I've observed that strong relationships have the opposite effect, where the support provided is a component of effective treatment of the disease. In my anecdotal experience, having a supportive partner makes a big difference in the patient's recovery. Simply having a spouse or family member who visits every day keeps the patient mentally strong, which translates into a quicker recovery.

Even in instances where the outcome was not "positive" (such as with Mr. and Mrs. Sanchez), these relationships make such a profound impact on the *quality* of life during their final days. Unfortunately, during the pandemic, we saw so many patients die alone. But we also saw many pass away surrounded by their loved ones. It is the latter who almost always feels fulfilled when their time comes.

Science seems to support the importance of loving relationships as well. There is a classic study indicating that married individuals experience generally far superior physical health than unmarried individuals.[39] Based on my experience with my patients, I suspect that this is likely due to committed partners looking out for each other's health or even advocating for each other. I often see patients come into the clinic with their spouse who will bring up issues of concern—such as their blood pressure at home or lack of exercise—that the patient themself will fail to.

Partners also hold each other accountable. In my experience, married patients are more likely to take their medications, come to their medical appointments, and adhere to an exercise or diet regimen. Researchers have even found that married couples were more likely to quit smoking than single individuals.[40]

An extensive scientific review on marriage found that married persons have significantly higher levels of happiness than persons who are not married. This effect was independent of financial and health-oriented protections offered by marriage.[41]

However, the strength and quality of the bond with one's spouse is of utmost importance. How close you are with your spouse *matters*. Researchers studying what factors promoted happiness in married couples did an extensive analysis, looking at seventeen different variables. They found that, by far, the strongest predictor of happiness was quality of marriage.[42]

Mr. and Mrs. Sanchez are an especially cute example of a couple who were truly best friends with each other, but I have noted that among my married patients who feel content with life during their final chapter, almost all consider their spouse to be their best friend, some literally referring to their spouse as such.

That doesn't necessarily mean you must have some incredible meet-cute or be childhood friends like José and Maria. Rather, it reflects the underlying mindset one brings to their marriage/relationship.

For instance, many of the patients I've cared for were actually married through an arranged marriage or through a process involving the families rather than the individuals. Nevertheless, among these patients who felt they lived fulfilled lives, they too considered their spouses to be their best friends.

In a rather extreme example, a couple whom I cared for in the hospital had gotten married through an arranged marriage process in India. Although their families knew each other, the two individuals did not know each other at all before getting married! Nonetheless, when I met them, they both excitedly referred to their partner as their best friend.

"We both went into the relationship with the mindset that this is the person I will be doing everything with. We worked to understand each other and to develop a reliable language of communication with each other," the husband shared with me. "After twenty years together, she is the person who matters most to me. Everything we do, we do together. I know what she thinks just by her eyes. She gives my life meaning."

Now, of course such an arrangement will not work for everyone, and culturally there are different approaches to marriage that work for different people. But I found the mindset toward the relationship to be both compelling and analogous to those I observed in the marriages of fulfilled patients, such as the Sanchezes.

Interestingly, there was a study done in India comparing arranged versus "love" (i.e., by choice) marriages. The researchers found that there was no significant difference in happiness between love-married couples and arranged-married couples. They did find that love-married couples can have better marital satisfaction when they have more freedom to select their own life partner compared to arranged marriage. Over all, the researchers concluded that love marriages and arranged marriages have their own merits and demerits.[43] The strength of the bond between the two spouses is what is important, regardless of the process.

At the end of the day, what matters is the understanding, trust, and love one has for their partner. Patients who exhibit the positive qualities exemplified by Maria and José Sanchez can't wait to spend time with their significant other, and being apart from them in the hospital breaks their heart.

Conversely, we've had patients who have expressed heart-wrenching confessions of regret that they never got to marry, as we found when we met Mr. Kensington.

A study done in the UK found that the well-being effects of marriage are about twice as large for those whose spouses are also their best friends. The researchers found that women benefit more from being married to their best friends than men do, but women are also less likely to regard their spouses as their best friend. Importantly, the scientists found that friendship was likely the mechanism that explained the causal relationship between marriage and life satisfaction.[44]

Of course, the idea of thinking of your partner in this manner is hardly a modern concept. Ancient traditions have described the value in treating your significant other as the other half of yourself. In Islam, there is a concept of literal soulmates where human beings are "created in pairs" and therefore "the best of you are those who are the best to their partner."[45]

Plato described that love is friendship that makes you feel complete in life. In his philosophical text "Symposium," Plato depicts a banquet where renowned men give a series of speeches, each one a metaphorical commentary on a larger philosophical point. During the banquet, comic playwright Aristophanes regales the other notable guests sitting at the table with a story depicting humans as being once created as creatures with four arms, four legs, and two faces. When they angered the Gods, Zeus struck the humans with his lightning, cutting each one in half! Since then, every human being has been missing their other half. Love, Plato noted, is the longing to find someone to join and become whole again.[46]

French existentialist philosopher and social theorist Simone de Beauvoir described love underpinned by close friendship as "authentic love." She noted that many of the marriages she observed in society during the early twentieth century were *inauthentic*, plagued by inequality and deprioritization of the other individual, or unrealistic exaltation that eventually burned out.

"An authentic love," wrote Beauvoir in her groundbreaking book *The Second Sex*, "should take on the other's contingence, that is, his lacks, limitations, and originary [sic] gratuitousness; it would claim to be not a salvation but an inter-human relation."[47]

De Beauvoir noted that there are many in relationships who have love in the absence of friendship, but that this leads to a far less fulfilling relationship as "[i]t makes you feel that you are simply an object of love, and not being loved for yourself alone."[48]

The COVID pandemic has inflicted death upon many, indiscriminately and without warning. Among those who are admitted to the hospital, the lucky ones have someone by their sides. Among those who die, the lucky ones have the one they love at their bedsides. Those with the fortune of experiencing the love of a life partner in their lifetime almost always express greater satisfaction with their lives to me as they die. My patients have taught me that marriage (or an equivalent partnership) with one's best friend is an important ingredient for a fulfilled life. Life is too short to miss out on such a meaningful companionship.

When our world inevitably ends and the final act of our life comes to a close, perhaps we can find solace in love, like Maria and José or the lovers of Pompeii.

Chapter 7
Discover the power of willpower.

Fredericksburg, Texas, in July. A burning Texas sun scorches the thick humid air, creating a sweltering atmosphere that would broil even the most hardened individual. As a California native, I found such heat borderline unbearable. During such summer days, I much prefer the refreshing coolness of the air conditioner, and I would not subject myself to be vulnerable to the blazing sun if it were not for a truly incredible opportunity. But this *was* a truly incredible opportunity, for eleven-year-old me was at the Texas elephant preserve, getting ready to meet *real-life elephants!*

"Now be careful and follow my lead. Asian elephants are gentle creatures, but they are very strong, so we need to make sure they do not feel threatened. In fact, their trunk is so strong that it can lift seven hundred and seventy pounds!" our guides told us as they took our group to meet the elephants. A simple, thin fence surrounded the preserve as we entered, beyond which stood a herd of majestic, gray elephants. It was truly a magical day where I got to meet and pet elephants—and even help give one a bath!

As the day drew to a close, I said goodbye to my new elephant friends and crossed the threshold of the thin fence, dwarfed in comparison to the impressive beasts contained within. I wondered to myself why the elephants never escaped. I felt bad for my new friends who were never allowed to leave their enclosure and roam free. Clearly, running through such a meager barrier should be nothing to them! There was nothing truly stopping them. Before I could dwell on this thought, my young brain was then quickly distracted by the gift shop where I insisted my parents buy me an elephant stuffed animal, and I would not revisit the thought until many years later.

Two decades later, I came across this same question while working as a physician at a skilled nursing facility (SNF). Both Mr. Harvey and Mr. Morganson were transferred to the same SNF when they were discharged from the hospital. They had almost identical medical histories and hospital courses such that it was easy to get them mixed up. It didn't help that their rooms were right next to each other too. They even looked very similar, both of them being eighty-year-old Caucasian men with silver stubble, glasses, and thin white hair.

They both had first experienced symptoms three weeks prior, which progressed to the point that they had gone to the hospital where they found out they had COVID. Although they had been at two different hospitals on opposite sides of downtown, they experienced similar hospital courses where their respiratory symptoms worsened over the first week, but reassuringly improved over the subsequent week.

Eventually they both were medically cleared to be discharged from the hospital. As we evaluate patients for discharge from the hospital, in addition to making sure they are medically ready for discharge, we also ensure they are physically safe to leave. This is particularly important for elderly patients who live independently before coming in.

Fighting an infection, such as COVID, in the hospital can cause patients to become quite weak. Physical and occupational therapists will often evaluate high-risk patients in the hospital to see if they are strong enough to be discharged home. If the patient is still weak and could benefit from additional therapy, the physical therapy team will recommend that they continue to work with therapists on an outpatient basis or that they be transferred to an SNF, where they can continue to undergo intensive physical therapy and occupational therapy.

Although both Mr. Harvey and Mr. Morganson had recovered from the infection, they were still quite weak physically, so their therapy teams recommended they go to a SNF where they could continue to undergo physical therapy until they were strong enough to go home. Up to this point, these two men had had parallel courses with journeys mirroring each other's, but their paths to recovery would drastically diverge.

As the first week at the SNF progressed, Mr. Harvey slowly regained his strength. During our morning rounds, the physical therapists would excitedly tell the medical team about Mr. Harvey's progress as his performance improved on their daily evaluations. The whole team was impressed at the incredible effort Mr. Harvey was putting into his exercises. He had the intensity of an Olympic athlete gunning for the gold, never losing focus and keeping his eye on the prize.

"I have to do the absolute best I can so I can recover and go back home to my family. I can't ever give up and have to overcome any hurdle," he told me one day as I examined him.

By the end of the week, he was able to ambulate independently and had regained almost all his strength. When we informed him that he was cleared for discharge, he was excited—literally able to jump up and down with glee!

After rounding on Mr. Harvey, we would round on Mr. Morganson, as he was in the next room in the hall. Alas, Mr. Morganson's progress was not quite as robust as Mr. Harvey's. The physical therapists who worked with him every day noted that they had to continuously encourage him to participate in his exercises. Even during the physical therapy sessions, the team was concerned he was not participating to his full ability and that this was hindering his recovery. By the end of the week, Mr. Morganson's performance on the physical therapist's evaluation was only minimally improved from when he first arrived.

As Mr. Harvey was packing his bags to leave the SNF, Mr. Morganson was still quite weak and bedbound. Both the medical team and physical therapist tried in vain to encourage Mr. Morganson to participate more actively in the physical therapies. We spent hours talking to him, trying to figure out why he was not actively participating as much as he could be.

"Doc, what's the point? I don't know if I'll ever get good enough to leave," he told us.

We told him that he could be, even giving examples of other patients (without any identifying details), with his same illness and level of function, who had been able to do so. We encouraged him to see a psychologist to perhaps improve his mental health as it may be impeding his progress, but he flatly refused.

Unfortunately, our efforts did not seem to have any effect.

Eventually, Mr. Morganson was discharged from the SNF to live with family members so they could actively support him.

The vastly divergent paths of Mr. Harvey's and Mr. Morganson's recoveries, despite their near identical initial presentation, is emblematic of a phenomenon that physicians and physical therapy teams often observe. In the mind/body duality, medical science emphasizes the body as we conceptualize the physiology and plan how we can optimize recovery in our patients. The oft-neglected half is the mind. Nonetheless, one's mental state has a profound influence on their physiologic state.

Although patients can be medically and physically identical, the willpower they possess has dramatic impacts on their recovery. Many in health care will note they have seen patients overcome incredible odds through grit and discipline in their recovery, while others have been unable to surmount far less.

This distinction has been quite evident during the COVID surges, during which many patients were discharged to SNFs once they were medically stable enough to leave the COVID wards. These patients were all sent to SNFs with very similar hospital courses, but had a variety of outcomes in terms of regaining their physical abilities. Of course, medical history and chronic conditions play a major role in how much one is able to recover from COVID, but there is significant emerging science on the role of willpower in recovering from severe illness.

Researchers in Norway have studied this by observing which characteristics were present in patients who had positive health outcomes after a hospitalization requiring being in the ICU. They found that these patients had strong "fighting spirits," which allowed them to reach even further than their prognoses predicted. Overall, they found family support and inner strength to be the two most critical factors for returning to a patient's ordinary life after a critical hospitalization.[49]

The importance of willpower is not limited to critically ill COVID patients. Ongoing research has shown willpower to be associated with general health. For example, researchers have found that willpower might be crucial for therapy success in diabetes patients.[50] I have observed the difference willpower can make in patients working to instill healthy habits to control their diabetes through lifestyle modification.

I see this often in my patients trying to lose weight. A common quality I've noted among my patients who have successfully achieved their weight loss goals is that they have a never-ending perseverance when faced with challenges and adversity, and they demonstrate great self-control when faced with temptation. As a physician, I try to support and foster these characteristics in my patients as well as be there as a form of support to fuel their willpower.

Psychologists have found that willpower has a major role to play in maintenance of weight loss, and health professionals could increase the effectiveness of weight management interventions through willpower enhancement.[51] As we think about the important medical therapeutics we prescribe to patients, it is important that health-care providers also foster the psychological qualities that will give patients the best chance of success.

Of course, the importance of willpower doesn't just apply to health-care patients. This has been the subject of a team of researchers at the University of Pennsylvania, led by psychology professor Angela Duckworth, who has been studying the importance of willpower and grit in life achievement. They evaluated schools around the nation to determine the underlying characteristics of successful students. They went to West Point military academy to see which cadets would drop out and which could hack it. They went to the national spelling bee to see who could make it to the final round.

Dr. Duckworth found that the successful individuals in these scenarios all had certain qualities in common: willpower and grit. They found that willpower and grit are associated with educational attainment. Among adolescents, more grit predicted a higher GPA and, inversely, fewer hours watching television. Among cadets at the United States Military Academy, West Point, increased willpower predicted retention. Among Scripps National Spelling Bee competitors, grit predicted ability to get to the final round.[52]

Importantly, science suggests that willpower is not just some metric you're born with; one's mindset toward it is what matters. The evidence suggests that simply *believing* you have willpower affects how you perform under pressure. For instance, when under stress of impending exams or of high stress/demand weeks, students who believed that willpower was a limited resource ate more unhealthy food (to help recover willpower), procrastinated more, reported more self-regulation failure, and obtained lower grades than those who believed they could recover their willpower.[53] What that means for us is that we should believe in ourselves, as each and every one of us has the willpower within us to overcome our most difficult obstacles. Having confidence in ourselves is what will unlock this untapped potential.

My anecdotal experience with my patients is consistent with this notion. I have found that health-care providers, family members, and other support systems can instill willpower into patients who are going through hurdles. Motivating patients to quit smoking or eat healthier is more effective when using encouraging, empowering language as well as making sure they have a strong support system to help the patient adhere to the behavioral change.

I had a patient who was addicted to alcohol. Every time he would come into the clinic for his yearly checkup, we would discuss how he should reduce his alcohol intake. And every year, he would tell me he'd try. But the number never went down.

One year, his lab tests showed his liver enzymes were creeping up higher than the last year. This was due to the large amount of alcohol intake causing fat deposits in the body of the liver. I advised him that if he did not quit drinking alcohol, he was at risk for his liver disease to progress to complete liver failure. I referred him to Alcoholics Anonymous as well as other resources to help him quit.

In our follow-up appointment six months later, he told me he had not had a drink in the previous five weeks. I asked how he had accomplished such an impressive feat when we had been struggling with this for years.

"I dug deep within myself to find the willpower to overcome this addiction. I knew I had to do it, so I could be here for my family," he told me.

I asked him what strategies he used so I could better counsel my other patients.

"I reframed the idea of failure. The first few weeks, I would relapse frequently. This was initially very discouraging. My sponsor told me that seeing failure as a devastating outcome would lead me astray, and instead I should take it as a learning opportunity and get right back to trying again."

He enthusiastically shared, "I let each victory fuel my enthusiasm. When faced with a temptation, I reminded myself of my goal so I could overcome it. And when I did overcome it, I would celebrate it. For the first month, I had to do this consciously, but overtime this became simply a part of my nature."

On the opposite end of the spectrum from willpower is a concept known as learned helplessness, which refers to patients accepting a sense of their own powerlessness.

And this brings us back to Fredericksburg, Texas, where a skinny barbed wire fence contains a herd of Asian elephants.

The psychologists who discovered the concept of learned helplessness actually did so by observing qualities in several animals, notably elephants. They asked the very same question pondered by many of us visiting zoos or elephant preserves—why don't elephants in captivity escape? After all, a fully grown elephant weighs over six tons, and the only thing keeping it in the enclosure is a thin chain that could easily snap.

Interestingly, they found that the reason is that the elephants in captivity have a mental block ingrained in their psychology. When the elephant is a baby, it is easily restrained to a small area with a thin chain leash. The little calf tries to escape to freedom many times, but every attempt at breaking out of the preserve is foiled by that thin chain. After many failed attempts, the baby elephant soon learns that escape is impossible. This belief becomes wired into its very brain and stays there as the elephant grows. Even when the elephant becomes big enough to easily break the chain and escape, it still retains the belief that it cannot escape!

Mr. Morganson's lack of confidence that he could improve is emblematic of learned helplessness and the impact it has on patients. Patients have *learned* they cannot improve on certain things. Even when their body may recover to the point that they can now regain certain abilities, their mind still believes these to be impossible. Learned helplessness has been associated with decreased mental health as well as unhealthy daily behaviors. Additionally, it is even thought to contribute to poorer outcomes in general diseases, such as lupus.[54]

The pandemic has shown patients and providers alike that we often cannot control the circumstances we are faced with, but we can control how we react to them. As Henry Ford said, "Whether you think you can, or you think you can't—you're right."[55]

My patients have taught me that approaching hurdles with willpower maximizes your chances of clearing them. These patients teach us to look at our own lives and ask ourselves, *What is it that I falsely believe I can't do, and how is this holding me back?* Just like the grown elephant tied to the chain, we have the strength within us to overcome many of the challenges we may find ourselves in. Our willpower can allow us to conquer feats we never knew were possible.

Chapter 8

Grow from guilt.

ealth-care workers have a love-hate relationship with Veterans Affairs (VA) hospitals, the nationalized health-care system in the United States specifically created to care for military veterans. Our patients at the VA have sacrificed for and served our nation, and it is truly an honor to care for them. It is a sad reality that the health conditions plaguing them are often a product of their service, such as those who develop COPD or PTSD. The veterans I cared for when I've worked at VA hospitals have been of unquestionable honor and unsurpassed kindness.

On the other hand, working at the VA makes you feel like you've gone back in time twenty years. Fax machines printing critical results and computers running Windows 98 are a staple of the physician workrooms. The electronic medical record (EMR) looks like software designed for the Commodore 64. Doctors wear physical pagers on their belts to receive important communication from nurses. Yet despite the Y2K-era technology, patient outcomes in the VA system are roughly equivalent to their private sector counterparts, which I believe is a testament to the dedication the staff at VA hospitals has to serving their patients.

Grant Hanson was a seventy-eight-year-old decorated Vietnam War veteran. As I examined him in the emergency room, his daughter proudly told me that he had been awarded honors for his service, but Mr. Hanson brushed it off, mumbling, "It's nothing."

He wore a simple button-down shirt and jeans and used a black cane to steady himself. Besides mentioning his service once during the initial history and physical—when he first came to the hospital with COVID symptoms—he did not mention it again after.

We agreed that we would watch his vitals over a few hours before deciding whether he was safe to go home. His breathing worsened over the day, and his oxygen levels remained borderline. When I checked in on him, I saw that he was wheezing while breathing, so we decided to admit him to the hospital to keep a close eye on him and start him on steroids and nebulized bronchodilators.

That night, I got a page from his nurse that he was getting delirious and was screaming at the nursing staff. Delirium is a sudden confusional state of altered consciousness in patients. It is common for elderly patients who are hospitalized, particularly when they have a degree of baseline dementia. The unfamiliar environment, as well as disruption in their sleep-wake cycle, can be disorienting for the patient and can lead to severe agitation and anxiety, particularly during the nighttime, a phenomenon that has been dubbed "sundowning."

When I got to the bedside, I saw Grant in the corner of the room. He was wide-eyed and nervously glancing around. Beads of sweat were rolling down his pale face.

"They're all back. They always come back. I'm so sorry!" he screamed at me when he saw me.

The best treatment of delirium in our patients is firstly preventing it from occurring. When we have elderly patients at high risk, we make sure they are physically active during the day and get adequate sleep at night. Physical therapy during the daytime and sleep hygiene after sunset are measures we try to maintain when we are able to in the hospital. These are good strategies for caring for the elderly and are generally healthy habits overall.

When patients become delirious, we first try nonpharmacological strategies. Compassionate reassurance, gentle touch, and reorientation are our first strategies. Family members or other familiar individuals can be very effective. When speaking to the patient, the delusions and hallucinations should not be endorsed nor challenged. If these initial strategies do not work, then we try medications. If the patient is a threat to themself or others, then physical restraints can be used as a last resort.

I carefully approached him and gently told him that he was safe and there was nobody else in the room.

"No, they're all here. Everyone I killed. I was just following orders! They'll always haunt me."

We were able to gradually calm down Grant with the help of his daughter, whom we called on the phone. He was able to sleep for the rest of the night. His daughter told us that even at home, he often had nightmares from his time in Vietnam.

Mr. Hanson was able to fight the infection over the next three days and was discharged from the hospital later that week. During that time, he had a couple more episodes of delirium, with similar hallucinations of those he had killed during his time in the military.

Similar situations of guilt racking one's mind are seen in many hospitalized combat veterans. Psychologists have found that guilt regarding combat experiences is an associated symptom of PTSD in military veterans. In studies, severity of guilt regarding combat was positively correlated with the reexperiencing and avoidance symptoms of PTSD and a general measure of PTSD severity.[56]

But this phenomenon is not limited to those who have seen combat. Disturbingly, doctors and nurses hear many stories of patients confessing decades-old crimes when delirious in the hospital or when suffering from dementia in old age. For most of our lives, we are able to suppress our thoughts and keep our secrets hidden with help from our frontal lobe, which serves as the filter for what makes it out of our innermost thoughts into our outer expressions. However, as we age, the frontal lobe loses its strength, and we are unable to suppress our thoughts as we were once able to.

The developing research in the field of neuroscience supports this, as the frontal lobe dysfunction results in deficits in dissociable capacities such as the direction of inhibition and sustained attention. Behaviorally, these deficits may be manifested as distractibility, neglect, and impulsivity.[57] Because this is also the part of the brain that declines with age, scientists have also determined a central role for frontal lobe dysfunction in memory loss and cognitive dysfunction of elderly people.[58] That is why it is not atypical for nurses who work in memory care units to have patients confess to old deeds or be racked with guilt on prejudiced actions from when they were young.

During the COVID pandemic, we saw many patients on their deathbeds either experience delirium characterized by guilt from prior actions or outright confess their guilt. Watching so many be unable to contain their shame and remorse during their final moments made it clear to me that we cannot outrun our conscience. Guilt is like a cancer that festers and eats away at one's conscience. Human beings may be able to stave away the inevitable outbreak by suppressing guilt deep into their subconscious with their frontal lobes, but this is only a temporary measure.

While the obvious lesson from these patients is to live our lives such that we do not feel any guilt in the first place, we have all done things we are not proud of. And while most of us may struggle with our guilt, particularly when we're older, there are some we have seen who were able to overcome this through *redemption*. And this does not need to be redemption of the religious kind, though that can be gratifying for some. A patient who really embodied this idea is Mrs. Hargreeves, whom I'd meet a month after treating Grant.

Mrs. Hargreeves grew up in a well-to-do family in the rural South. She grew up with strong traditional "family values." She described to me that the prevailing sentiment in her town was that the country was being overrun by immigrants. As is human nature, she internalized this viewpoint. She and her husband supported politicians and organizations that claimed to defend America's "White tradition." Ashamed, she told me that her father had even gone to a Klan rally once.

But as fate would have it, their daughter befriended an African American boy at school. Through their daughter, they got to know this boy and his family, realizing that their view of people of color had been clouded by lies and prejudice.

Mrs. Hargreeves and her family began supporting civil rights organizations to undo the damage they had done in their ignorance, becoming active members and donors to the NAACP and the ACLU.

By the time I met Mrs. Hargreeves, her husband had been deceased for almost a decade. She had an especially aggressive variant of COVID, and within the week, it was clear she was not going to make it.

As she lay on the hospital bed, taking her final breaths, she was surrounded by her daughter and her son-in-law (the same boy her daughter befriended when they were little!). She held her daughter's and son-in-law's hands through the COVID gown and gloves. Between breaths, she thanked them and God for a life worth living.

And then she passed away.

Guilt without redemption will eat away at you until the very end. But acknowledgment of one's guilt and working to redeem oneself can lead to fulfillment.

Chapter 9

Stand, even if you stand alone.

Andre Abara was eighty-seven years old when he came into the hospital after having high-grade fevers and trouble breathing. It was the peak of the first COVID surge in Southern California, and he was worried that he may have been exposed.

Mr. Abara was a dwarf due to a condition called achondroplasia. He had stunted legs and used a cane to walk due to severe arthritis of his left knee. As he sat on the chair, his legs hung over the edge, barely touching the ground. His South African accent and baritone voice made him sound like a narrator for the latest action blockbuster, and he spoke with a slow, purposeful cadence that made you latch on to every word. His curly gray hair and a neatly trimmed beard gave him a look of distinction while his light brown eyes with subtle spark displayed both kindness and boldness.

The evening sun shining through the window cast a golden glow behind Mr. Abara, giving the appearance of a halo surrounding his head. As I walked through the door, it shone into my eyes, causing me to squint. Using his cane, he stood up to greet me when I entered the room. He smiled, put both hands over his heart, and gave me a small bow. When he stood, he blocked the sun's bright beam, casting a long shadow across the room, easing the harsh glare and making it much easier for me to see.

"So good to meet you doctor. I would shake your hand, but best not considering COVID, eh?"

I showed him that his oxygen levels were borderline and that he would be admitted to the hospital if his COVID test were positive so that we could initiate treatments and therapeutics. Mr. Abara had a condition called liver cirrhosis, in which the liver becomes permanently scarred and no longer functions. Because of this, he was at high risk for infections and would need a thorough workup. Additionally, any infection he may have (such as COVID) could easily become quite severe as cirrhosis can weaken the body's defenses and immune system. He also had a history of lung cancer. Although it was now in remission after chemotherapy, his history still meant that he would be particularly susceptible to a worsening lung infection.

In order to clarify his code status, I tenderly asked him if he would like CPR done if he were to pass away.

"Can I tell you something I am very proud of in my life?" he asked me rather than answering the question.

"Of course," I responded.

"When I was fifteen, I was in school. During our lunch break, I loved playing with my friends in the yard. Out of the corner of my eye, I saw a group of kids kicking another boy who was laying on the ground. He was crying and they were calling him *moffie*." (Moffie is a South African slur for a gay person).

He clasped his hands together and shifted his attention to the window as he recalled this story from his childhood.

"There was blood in his nose, and his right eye was hurt. He had curled himself into a ball. I stopped my game and ran over to the group, asked them why they were doing this. They told me that this boy was gay. The teacher in the schoolyard was not doing anything. The teacher saw this was going on, but turned the other way."

His eyes began filling up, and he sniffed to clear his nose. I handed him a tissue so that he could blow his nose.

"I had been bullied a lot as a child for being a dwarf. The pain that comes with being rejected by society is no stranger to me. So, I ran in, grabbed the boy, and tried to take him to his home. Nobody was there to support him, including the teachers. The boys had started to yell and even threw things at me as well. But I knew I had to do what was right.

"It turned out to be the best thing that I'd ever done. You see, unbeknownst to me, a girl had watched me do this. She went up to me a few weeks later and told me I was brave for doing the right thing. Ten years later, I ended up marrying her. We would eventually immigrate to America, and now here we are.

"I share this with you because I have always tried to live my life to do what is right. My mother always told me that I must have the bravery to walk alone as long as I am walking on the right path. Doing this has given me a great sense of purpose in life. It has also given me much joy. Learning from my wife, who shares my values, and imparting these values to my children has been the distinction of my life."

As he continued, his voice felt like it was becoming even deeper as if to somehow reflect the gravity of his words. "If I die, then I will die with happiness to have lived the life I've had. Do not try to bring me back if I am dead. My wife died seven years ago from cancer, and she was ready for death then, just as I am now. I am ready for death if it is to come for me."

Andre Abara would not survive the hospitalization. His breathing worsened. In four short days, he was on a maximum high-flow nasal cannula and gasping for air. He was transitioned to comfort care measures so that we could make sure his final moments in life were not with pain.

The bravery to do what is right, even if standing alone, is a common quality I have observed in many patients who have led meaningful lives. Some have done exceptional deeds in the realms of civil rights, community service, or scientific research. I have met patients who have advocated for social justice in scenarios where it would make them despised. I have met scientists who went against the convention of the field to discover novel methods of uncovering life's secrets.

But equally significant, or perhaps more so, are the patients who have instilled moral courage into their daily lives. The ones who stand up for what is right in their social circles, even if their beliefs are unpopular. Those who stand up against bigotry, even if it is displayed by those they love. And those who stand up for their partners, families, or loved ones against others.

Doing so comes with risk. This is evident in the dramatic examples of civil rights leaders and social justice advocates. As author Kelseyleigh Reber wrote, "When we stand up for what we believe in—for what's right—there is always a chance that we risk the very things we fight for: our safety, our lives, our freedom. But if we stand down, the risk is definite."[59]

Persisting for what is right when alone is never risk-free, even for those of us who may be doing so on a smaller scale. Standing up for one's principles is difficult, especially when we do so against those we like, such as our friends and family. We can even risk these relationships by doing so. Having the honesty and integrity to stand up not only adds authenticity to the relationship and makes each person better for it, it can actually make the relationship deeper. This nuance is the difference between hanging out with "yes men" who agree with everything you say, and with someone who supports you but will also call you out when needed.

Psychologists have termed this "stand-up" quality as moral courage. Moral courage is the ability to overcome fear and stand up for one's values: "It is the willingness to speak out and do that which is right in the face of forces that would lead a person to act in some other way. It puts principles into action."[60]

This is not a novel concept, of course. Aristotle believed that moral courage is the foundation on which lies the rest of human qualities because it is the quality that guarantees the opportunity for development of more sophisticated character traits. It is the prerequisite to living a life of morality.[61] Ancient Athenian general Thucydides wrote, "The secret to happiness is freedom ... and the secret to freedom is courage."[62]

In the business world, leaders who are shown to possess moral courage are shown to be more authentic leaders. Furthermore, those who worked under these leaders had more ethical behaviors.[63] Health-care workers with greater moral courage have even been posited to have better patient outcomes and save more lives.[64]

This pandemic has shown us a very practical example of how everyday implementation of moral courage can literally save lives. When COVID-19 first spread to the United States, the CDC recommended social distancing guidelines in order to curb the spread of the disease, particularly to the most vulnerable. The cases we would see in the wards or ICU were often of those where the patient or a loved one did not practice safe social distancing practices, or those around them did not wear a mask. In certain communities, wearing a mask and social distancing was likely not the popular action and required moral courage to do. Among those with certain extreme political leanings as well as young adults, adhering to social distancing guidelines could prompt ridicule. Political leaders and media personalities openly mocked or expressed disdain for the CDC guidelines. But even in such an environment, many were brave and still insisted on social distancing.

Studies have shown that social distancing is projected to have likely saved *millions of lives* in the US as well as resulted in an economic benefit of roughly $60,000 per household.[65] The year 2020 was truly a remarkable time where one could be a hero and save a life simply by staying at home.

This effect was again demonstrated with the COVID vaccine. Political interest groups, social networking apps, and fringe media propagated blatant misinformation about the vaccine and openly scorned efforts to get the population vaccinated. Of course, almost all of my patients who died with COVID after the vaccine was released were unvaccinated. On the other hand, I have had patients who initially did not want to get vaccinated. However, they had a loved one who was brave to stand up to them and convince them to get vaccinated. A few individuals even took a stance, saying they would not come see them until they were vaccinated. Then, when their loved one got COVID, the vaccination literally saved their life.

Luckily, moral courage is something we can develop! Researchers have shown that counterintuitively, moral courage is actually something that can be learned. It is a skill or muscle that can be strengthened over time. Simply learning about moral courage and reading about examples in history or life where it has resulted in heroism can help us develop our own moral courage. Significantly, the most effective way to develop one's own moral courage is by simply being around other individuals who demonstrate moral conduct in the face of difficult circumstances.[66]

Patients like Andre Abara have taught me that instilling the virtue of moral courage into my daily life can lead to a fulfilling life. Although it can manifest itself in heroic acts, like in Mr. Abara's story, moral courage also has its role in standing up for our values in our day-to-day lives.

It is easy to live our lives assimilating with what is popular, but the popular opinions can be transient. This is often the case when those opinions are *wrong*. As Martin Luther King, Jr. reminds us, "The arc of the moral universe is long, but it bends toward justice."[67]

I have met many patients who have regretted not standing up for what was right, but have yet to meet someone who had regretted doing so, even if they were alone.

Suzy Kassem, Egyptian-American writer, poet, and philosopher wrote, "Stand up to hypocrisy. If you don't, the hypocrites will teach. Stand up to ignorance, because if you don't, the ignorant will run free to spread ignorance like a disease. Stand up for truth. If you don't, then there is no truth to your existence. If you don't stand up for all that is right, then understand that you are part of the reason why there is so much wrong in the world."[68]

Chapter 10

Do not care what the people say.

When Adithi Patel first was told she had tested positive for COVID, the sixty-nine-year-old Indian American first turned to her husband, Sandeep, and said, *"Log kya kahenge?"* ("What will people think?"). This is a common phrase in Urdu and Hindi used in the Indian subcontinent to create fear of the public's opinion on one's life. Most individuals in South Asia (or with a *desi* ethnic background) will have heard this phrase commonly said, and it was Mrs. Patel's first thought when she developed symptoms.

Mrs. Patel had first started experiencing a cough and trouble breathing a few days after attending a large wedding. She showed me pictures on her phone of a lavish wedding taking the span of multiple days (which can be typical of desi weddings). Vibrant colors, sparklers, and an array of sweets set a breathtaking backdrop to the festivities. She swiped through photos of flashy dances and glamorous saris. There seemed to be only a handful of people there wearing masks.

"I know it is not recommended by the government to go to these social functions due to COVID, but you must understand, we have to think about our social obligations as well."

We discussed that we would monitor her oxygen level overnight and use that to determine whether she should be hospitalized. When I checked in on her, Mrs. and Mr. Patel were deep in discussion on whether they should inform their social circle and family. They had drafted several iterations of WhatsApp messages and were carefully editing them before sending. It was clear that a whole public relations campaign was in progress.

As I got to know them over the course of the night, I learned that their son, Devon, had recently become engaged. Weddings are a very big affair in South Asian culture, oftentimes spanning several events over the course of a week. Devon and his fiancée did not want a big event. They wanted to do a virtual wedding online with a small event with close family after the pandemic, as that made sense for their personal financial situation and was consistent with their sense of social responsibility in the midst of the pandemic.

"That is not how our culture works!" Mrs. Patel exclaimed with an exasperated sigh as she ranted with me. "You must do this for your prestige in the community. Or else what will they think of him and his ability to provide? *Log kya kahenge?*"

Mr. Patel nodded in agreement.

Mrs. Patel's symptoms stayed stable, so we discharged her home with instructions to quarantine and return if her symptoms were to worsen.

A week later, I saw Mr. Sandeep Patel in the emergency room. I didn't recognize him at first, but he reminded me how I had treated his wife the previous week. He had started experiencing similar symptoms a few days later. He initially hoped his condition would improve like his wife's symptoms did, but the night before, he had begun to have significant difficulty. Unfortunately, since his wife was still in her quarantine period, she could not join him at the hospital.

His oxygen levels were low, so we started oxygen at a low level via nasal cannula and admitted him into the hospital. As I was initiating the process of admitting him and organizing the therapeutics, I noticed he was on a FaceTime call with his wife on his iPad. While not intending to eavesdrop, I again overheard the phrase, *"Log kya kahenge?"*

Mr. Patel's condition worsened over the next three days. Eventually, he was on maximum settings on high-flow nasal canula (HFNC), but his oxygen levels were not able to keep up. As the infection progressed, his organs began to fail. His mental status also declined dramatically, but he would have periods of mental lucidity, particularly when his wife was able to visit him (she was now outside the quarantine period).

One afternoon when I came in to assess him, he told me he had something very important to tell me. Beads of sweat were pouring down his forehead, and his eyes appeared bloodshot. He was trembling as he grabbed my arm and said, "We have lived our whole lives thinking about what people will think. It has shaped our careers, social circles, and the way we brought up our children. But none of those people are here now. Most of them have not even bothered to give me a phone call."

His wife, sitting next to him, held his hand. Even through the N95 mask and PPE, I could see she had tears in her eyes.

"How foolish it seems now. I've cared about the opinions of people I don't even like, sometimes even putting strain on my relationships with those I love," Mrs. Patel quietly said.

This realization is one I've seen many patients make at their deathbeds. Humans are social beings and therefore become concerned about what others will think. We are predisposed to think about our place in social hierarchies. It is only when one's impending mortality thrusts perspective upon us that we realize how unimportant overthinking others' perception of us is.

Social scientists and neuroscientists have elucidated the neural mechanisms that underpin this cognitive bias. They have found that overthinking the opinion of others impairs people's ability to take appropriate action. Caring less about what others think, on the other hand, may help to deactivate inhibitory pathways in our brain, and this may be conducive to people doing the right thing.[69]

This is, of course, hardly a novel concept. Stoic philosopher Seneca said, "How mad is he who leaves the lecture-room [sic] in a happy frame of mind simply because of applause from the ignorant! Why do you take pleasure in being praised by men whom you yourself cannot praise?"[70]

Many of my patients who have come to this realization have expressed regret at trying to impress individuals they don't even know. With the advent of social media, I've had patients who are critically ill reveal anguish at caring about social media "likes" from people who they themselves don't even like!

Additionally, psychologists have long known that how an individual reacts to you reflects upon them rather than you. Carl Jung referred to this phenomenon as projection, which occurs when we attribute an aspect of our own personalities or thoughts to another person. Carl Jung wrote, "Projection is one of the commonest psychic phenomena .... Everything that is unconscious in ourselves we discover in our neighbor, and we treat him accordingly."[71]

Patients who experience a close brush with death will sometimes describe to me that they have gained a perspective that they are not the center of the universe. This seems like a rather obvious thing to say (*Hamza, I don't need to nearly die to tell you I'm not the center of the universe!*), but we often live our lives as if we are. We live as if other people are constantly talking about us and it is so important to live by what they are saying.

I had a patient, Donald Stenson, whom you will meet in a few chapters, who came back to life after his heart stopped beating.

"When I was lying there, watching you all do CPR on me from the beyond, I realized the world does not revolve around me. I should not be so prideful to hold hatred and fear in my heart. Rather than worrying about what other people think about me, I should just do what will bring happiness and peace into my life. I cannot control what others do and think, so I should not let it control my life," he said to me when I visited him after his ICU course.

Scores of patients have expressed regret at being preoccupied with what "society" thinks of them during their lives. I've observed many make completely irrational decisions purely to impress others. Strangely, many will cripple the actually important relationships, such as with their spouses or close friends, in order to impress an abstract concept of greater society. Those who spend their time trying to impress others often find that despite their efforts to obtain their social standing, they have not developed any deep relationships. In fact, psychologists and therapists from as far back as the 1970s have proven in studies that prioritizing your spouse's feelings over the opinions of others results in a far healthier relationship.[72]

Against all odds, Mr. Patel began to turn a corner the next day. His breathing improved, and he required less oxygen support to breathe. Two days later, he did not require any oxygen support to breathe.

I got an email in my inbox a few months later. It was a Zoom link to Devon's wedding, where I got to witness a beautiful ceremony with their family and a few close friends. There were still vibrant colors, sparklers, and an array of sweets to set a breathtaking backdrop to the festivities. Through the computer, I enjoyed the flashy dances and glamorous saris. But at this event, everyone was carefully social distancing and wearing masks (that matched the vivid colors of the saris!). At the end of the virtual event, I got to speak to Mr. and Mrs. Patel. Their faces were full of joy.

"Log jo kahenge, kahenge. Mein kyu fikar karhu? Hum khush hai." (People will say what they say. Why should we worry? We are happy.)

Chapter 11

Live with "Bright Energy, Careful Planning"

D r. Hatake was known throughout his Veterans Affairs Hospital for his unshakable calmness no matter what came through the door—an extremely valuable trait for an emergency medicine physician. A physician in his seventies, he was actively involved in Doctors Without Borders and health-care advocacy, and he had started his career by being at the forefront during the AIDS epidemic, later going through SARS, H1N1, and now COVID-19.

His pristine and pressed white coat, always lined with buttons advocating movements in health-care justice and advocacy from different eras of the past few decades, had the appearance of a military general's.

"This isn't my first rodeo, good doctor!" he enjoyed exclaiming to his medical students at the start of the COVID-19 pandemic.

During the first COVID surge, the morale in the hospital was at an all-time low. Technically, the hospital was at 120 percent capacity— makeshift rooms had been created to allow for greater capacity than the hospital was designed for—and everyone was exhausted from the endless barrage of COVID-positive patients being admitted. And, since this was the first surge, there was great uncertainty as to how to treat patients, given that there was not enough data to predict how effective the treatment strategies would be.

Despite all this, nobody ever saw Dr. Hatake let out even so much as a sigh. Moreover, he elevated the mood of his entire team when times were darkest. His light personality was accentuated by his floral shirts and a cheesy poster on his desk that read: "Every day may not be good, but there is something good in every day."

"This too shall pass! No matter how bad things get, the sun will come up and we will go home in the morning. As long as we are doing right by our patients and healing them to the best of our ability, then we should always look upon our work with pride, no matter the outcome. Bright energy!" he was often heard telling his trainees at 1 a.m. during the night shift.

But that did not mean he was ignorant to the realities of the situation. Dr. Hatake was no prescriber of toxic positivity. Rather, he deliberately thought through the worst-case scenarios, planning on how he could deal with them. He warned medical residents and helped medical groups formulate response teams to the pandemic before the first surge began, just in case it got that bad.

"You must purposefully think through how you will overcome the hurdles coming your way. Think about what can go wrong, and think what you'll do then. You'll find that careful planning will help make sure you remain with bright energy no matter how dark it gets!" he told his medical students during rounds.

His optimism never wavered. His planning never faltered.

"I respect myself too much to let pessimism take over. By always thinking of the best in others and never losing a sense of hope, I'll always be able to rest at night," he'd say with a wink, followed by his catchphrase, "Bright energy, careful planning!"

It was surreal to walk into the emergency room and see Dr. Hatake in a patient room rather than in the bullpen. I had the same feeling of uneasiness I'd have as a kid when seeing a teacher at a grocery store.

"My usual seat was taken!" he joked when I greeted him after putting on my N95 mask.

Just as the first wave of the pandemic was slowing down, Dr. Hatake began experiencing symptoms. Being high-risk, he got tested right away and found he was positive. He was having great difficulty breathing and was not able to maintain his oxygen level without support, so he was admitted into the hospital.

Nurses, doctors, medical students, and housekeeping staff would all give Dr. Hatake a wave through the window when walking by his room. In turn, he would give them a thumbs up and a wink. The whole hospital was rooting for him.

Over the next four days, Dr. Hatake's breathing continued to worsen. He was transitioned up from a nasal cannula to a HFNC. We continued to aggressively treat his respiratory status with the appropriate therapeutics, but despite that, his settings on the high-flow needed to be steadily increased over the next day. Eventually he was on the maximum amount of oxygen support able to be provided by HFNC.

That evening, his oxygen numbers decreased. When I went to his room to assess him, we discussed that the next step would be intubation and using a ventilator to oxygenate his lungs. Although I had had this discussion with many patients, it felt quite odd having it with Dr. Hatake, one of my mentors. He knew far better than me what our next step was, as well as the implication this had on his chances of making it out of the hospital.

He nodded. I could tell he had already thought of this before I entered the room.

"I understand. I am hopeful that I will be able to make it through this, although I know the odds are not in my favor. I'd like to video chat with my son one last time before you intubate me," he said.

He paused for a second. And then he gave me his trademark wink and thumbs up.

I was taken aback by his positivity, even in this dire situation. Despite the N95 and PPE, it must have been apparent on my face.

"You are surprised that I can remain so optimistic, even when I am about to be put on a ventilator, eh? Well, optimism is not naivety. I am not foolishly blind to the dark realities of our world, or our job. I choose to focus on the good in the world and to always hold out hope.

"If we let pessimism take hold, then we are closing the door to progress, solutions, and a better future. That is the difference between naivety and purposeful optimism, my friend. You manifest your own reality. The energy you put into your life, be it positive or negative, will shape your actions, which in turn will shape the future," he said, smiling softly, each sentence interrupted with a deep breath.

Science supports Dr. Hatake's philosophy, as researchers have found that optimism increases the ability to deal with stressors effectively and causes many successful health outcomes.[73] Importantly, the latest research indicates that just as Dr. Hatake noted, blind optimism alone can be counterproductive. Rather, one must have positive thoughts, but also be aware of the negativity and difficulties they will encounter.[74]

In scientific literature, optimism appears to be associated with higher levels of subjective well-being, better health, and more career success.[75] Having a positive outlook even allows one to live longer, as studies have shown that optimistic outlook appears to be a significant predictor of survival among the elderly.[76]

These studies highlight the importance for health-care professionals to cultivate positive mental health in addition to physical health in their patients, as the latest research supports that the two are linked.

This lesson in optimism is one we should incorporate into our own lives as health-care providers, particularly during such times when our job can involve seeing the darkest in humanity. Psychologists have found that optimism and proactive coping when dealing with work-related stresses have a positive impact on quality of life for nurses.[77]

Many of the lessons we've learned so far, as well as those we will learn with patients later in this book, offer effective strategies in helping one get through difficult times and improve one's quality of life. When going through a hardship, focusing on the temporary nature of that hardship helps give us an important perspective. Knowing that *this too shall pass* gives us the strength to overcome whatever hurdle life throws at us. Additionally, instilling a sense of gratitude in our mindfulness practices will train our minds to always identify the silver lining in life.

It is also paramount to generally believe in good in others and the world. Human beings are generally good, and Dr. Martin Luther King Jr. was right—"the arc of the moral universe is long, but it bends toward justice." Scientists have actually found that belief in the good in others and that the world is a just place is associated with better mental health and overall optimism.[78] I often have trouble with the latter, as it can be difficult to believe the world is just when we see so much injustice everywhere we look. As a doctor, I have witnessed the injustice of our very own health-care system, much of which has been aggravated during the pandemic. With the globalization of information, we are now privy to (some of) the immense suffering experienced by many around the world.

It is easier to believe in the overall goodness of humanity, however. Even where there is immense suffering and injustice, there are good people working to help others. As Fred Rogers famously said, "Look for the helpers. You will always find people who are helping."

"Bright energy"—*deep breath*—"careful planning!" Dr. Hatake whispered.

An hour later, we intubated Dr. Hatake. Despite our best efforts, his status continued to deteriorate over the next few weeks, leading to multiorgan failure. Eventually, he passed away. All the staff on the ward, from food delivery to respiratory therapist, looked somber.

The charge nurse looked around, then stood on her chair to address everyone.

"It's okay to feel sad right now. Dr. Hatake represented the best in us. But before we start letting this get us down, remember what Dr. Hatake taught us. No matter how dark it gets, we must focus on hope. Bright energy, careful planning!"

The mood shifted. I picked up my next patient's chart. It is important to not be blind to the realities of our world, but it is just as important to always hope for the best future. That's what Dr. Hatake taught us.

Chapter 12

You can learn something from everyone.

Luke Williams's eyes lit up whenever he spoke about his neighborhood on the South Side: "Everywhere you look, you see people *living*. My street has aunties making the best soul food in their diners and cousins with auto shops who are truly dedicated to their craft. The streets have oldheads and kids alike enjoying the day. Our teachers make do with the little they get in order to create a brighter tomorrow for our kids. It's *good people!*"

Luke Williams had dedicated his whole life to working with at-risk youth in the South Side. He had grown up in the projects in this very same neighborhood that he now served. He told me how in his twenties and thirties, he had started running with, in his words, "a tough, up-to-no-good crew."

"There isn't always a support system for the youth in these neighborhoods, and these gangs can be the only outlet they have for a sense of community and belonging. That's what happened to me."

This behavior led to him being arrested and spending three years in jail.

"It's the best thing that ever happened to me!" he told me with a smile.

I was surprised and asked him how so.

Luke explained that in jail, he'd had a self-awakening where he realized that he had been wasting his life. He met a chaplain who would visit the prison regularly and taught him the value of mindfulness, ethics, and social justice. Inspired, Luke began studying social work in the prison library.

"Being in the system became my crucible. I looked around and saw individuals who had been in and out of the system for so long, they did not know how to be back in society, let alone be a force of positivity for their community. I decided that when I'd get out, I'd help my neighborhood."

After being released, Luke completed his degree in social work at the local community college in the same neighborhood where he grew up. He started working at nonprofit organizations that provided support to his community.

The day I met Luke, he had been working at a nonprofit organization that functioned both as a food bank providing meals to the needy and as a resource center for individuals who had recently finished paying their debts to society.

Unfortunately, due to limited food supply, that week they had been having to strictly limit the maximum amount they could give to each household, which had caused a lot of frustration for some of the people he was trying to support.

During one shift, two men in ski masks walked in brandishing knives. They swung at Luke, inflicting large wounds on his arm and chest. They then took all the donation boxes full of cash as well as several boxes of food.

I met Luke in the emergency department where he came in to have his wounds treated after this event. After hearing what had brought him in, I couldn't help but feel disheartened.

"Wasn't it discouraging to be attacked by the very people you're trying to help?" I asked him.

"It's not the first time something like this has happened. And yes, it can be at times," he responded. "But I learned in prison that everyone you encounter in life can teach you something. Everyone you meet knows something you don't know. Their actions teach you these lessons to help you grow. And the onus is on you to learn from them with an open mind."

"But what lesson can be found in such a senseless act of violence?" I asked him.

"Senseless? Those two men taught me today that there is such hunger in my community, people are willing to risk their lives and dignity for a couple boxes of food," Mr. Williams softly said while shaking his head.

Then he looked up at me and added, "And they taught me to not forget to lock the doors after hours!" with a chuckle.

I carefully cleaned Luke Williams's wounds and stitched up the particularly long gash on his arm. By that time, the basic lab work drawn started coming back.

I got a call from the pathologist, the doctor who specializes in, amongst other things, expertly analyzing cells under the microscope. She told me there were severe irregularities in Mr. Williams's white blood cells that could be consistent with acute myeloid leukemia (AML), a type of cancer of the blood cells.

When I shared this with Luke, I expected him to be shocked. After all, he had come in to get his wounds treated and now was finding out he may have cancer.

He took a deep breath after I finished gently explaining the results and their implications. "I understand, doc. There will be a lesson in this as well that I must learn."

I did not see Mr. Williams in person after he left that day, as much of his health care was now done at the oncology center at a different campus. But we kept in touch via email. During the later COVID surges, when people would protest the lockdown by picketing the hospital building, he took the time to reach out to me.

He explained to me that it is easy to dismiss people, particularly when their actions or viewpoints are in direct contradiction with your own. It is much harder to understand where they are coming from.

"You always have to ask yourself questions to understand their perspective. What does this individual know, that I do not know, that is shaping their views? What has this person experienced in life that has caused them to think the way that they think?

"That does not mean you will end up agreeing with them, however!" Luke added. "The goal is not for everyone to agree. That'd be too boring. The goal is for us all to be able to better understand each other and learn from each other."

I went through this struggle for understanding later that year, when during the Omicron COVID surge, we were overrun with an influx of patients who had refused vaccination and now had gotten COVID. Being dismissive of these individuals as illiterate or dumb is easy—and also inaccurate. With Mr. Williams's words echoing in my head, I took the time to learn where they were coming from.

Some anti-vax patients cited the United States's history of experimenting on people of color. Others described that their elders had advised them not to get vaccinated, and they respected their wisdom. And yes, others were convinced that Bill Gates was trying to put microchips in their blood, though their numbers were far fewer than social media will have you believe.

I found that by understanding their perspectives and learning from them, I was able to better help my patients achieve their personal health goals in a way that aligned with their values. For example, I acknowledged the tragic history of our nation's systemic injustice toward African Americans. I also shared how COVID vaccination rates were lower among people of color, which was leading to poorer outcomes during the pandemic for these communities. A few people were convinced to be vaccinated, but regardless, we all definitely developed a better understanding of each other.

Well, perhaps not the Bill Gates conspiracy community yet, but I'm getting there ....

Many other patients shared a similar philosophy to Luke Williams's. I cared for a patient who was an executive at a large company. She recounted how she took this lesson in understanding quite literally and kept a journal where she would write lessons taught to her from employees she'd meet at her company.

"Every single person in the company knows more about at least one part of the business than I do, although I imagine that's a conservative estimate," she said. "Ever since I started this journaling habit, I've found that I've developed a more intricate and practical understanding of our process and am able to better conceptualize how certain management initiatives will affect our manufacturing and distribution workers. Most managers have only a theoretical understanding of the practical details, and that's why so many ideas that come down from the top never really pan out the way you'd think!" she exclaimed as she flipped through her notebook, showing me various points she had learned from those around her.

"A lot of executives are so far up their ass that they'd rather pay an exorbitant amount of money to a consulting firm to wait five months to learn something that the gentleman manning the front desk in the lobby already knew—just from his observations!"

As Ralph Waldo Emerson wrote in his letters in the 1800s: "Shall I tell you the secret of the true scholar? It is this: Every man I meet is my master in some point, and in that I learn of him."[79]

There are, of course, some people who are simply too far gone or vile with hatred and prejudice in their hearts. Ignorance has corroded their perspectives, and their lives are devoid of any productivity or compassion. When I brought that up with Mr. Williams, he chuckled and responded with, "Keep an open mind. You will learn lessons from surprising sources. Though, with some people you may simply learn what *not* to do. They may be the type of people from whom all you learn is patience or forbearance."

I have met many who have taught me to suffer fools gladly and engender patience with politeness.

A year later, I received an email from Mr. Williams's oncologist that he had passed away due to a complication of his disease. He told me Luke wanted to express his gratitude for everything he had learned from me and to tell me to keep learning from everyone I meet.

Inspired by Luke Williams, I began writing the lessons I learned through my experiences as a physician. As the pandemic raged on, certain themes began emerging as I continued to take notes. Those lessons would eventually serve as the foundation for this book.

Chapter 13

Follow your own dreams.

What is your dream?

I feel like I have a pretty good idea of what my dreams are, but sometimes I struggle with answering that question, and the following one: *Am I following my dreams?* Patients on their deathbeds do not struggle to tell me what their dreams were, however. I imagine this lack of ambivalence is part and parcel of the clarity of reflection thrust upon you in the final chapter of your life. The lucidity of mortality also makes it abundantly clear to us whether we pursued our dreams during our lives, or whether we ended up working toward the dreams of others.

At age fifty-five, Nicole Lin had been working at a large Silicon Valley tech giant for over two decades when she first was diagnosed with breast cancer. She was immediately referred to an oncologist, and after the initial staging studies and confirmatory testing, she began chemotherapy.

Chemotherapy is a double-edged sword, as the same drug that prevents cancer cells from rapidly dividing also stops cells that naturally require rapid division. Chemotherapy prevents the body from generating new cells. This can be obvious with the commonly experienced hair loss or skin deterioration with those starting chemotherapy. A clinically significant ramification of this side effect is that the white blood cells, which are the immune cells tasked with fighting infections, begin to rapidly decrease in number as new ones are unable to replace old ones.

Due to this reality, cancer patients receiving chemotherapy are considered to be immunocompromised and are counseled to come to the hospital should they experience even the slightest sign of an infection, such as the beginnings of a fever.

When Nicole began experiencing fevers and difficulty breathing, she came into the emergency room later that same day after calling her oncologist's clinic. She tested positive for COVID-19. Unfortunately, this was before the COVID vaccine had been approved. She was admitted to the hospital for close monitoring given her immunocompromised state.

Nicole grew up in New York City and came out West to go to college at Stanford, where she majored in journalism. She dreamed of one day being an investigative journalist for the *Wall Street Journal* or *New York Times*. When she told her parents, they did not see the practicality in her dreams.

"We're not spending our whole savings on your education so you can maybe work for a newspaper, Nicole. Find a respectable professional job with good job security, like computer science," her mother told her.

So, after graduating, she went on to pursue her master's in computer science at the University of California at Berkeley.

COVID progressed quite rapidly in Nicole due to the chemotherapy affecting her immune system and making her susceptible to concurrent infections with both bacteria and COVID. To make matters worse, the cancer had metastasized to her lungs, making her pulmonary health already compromised.

By the second day, she needed to be put on BiPAP, which is a mask that actively helps you breathe. Similar to HFNC, BiPAP is considered one of the maximum supports for oxygenation that can be provided before intubation and being attached to a ventilator.

That evening when I rounded on Nicole's room to assess her status, she was crying. She shared with me that although she knew she was incredibly lucky to live the life she had led, she felt regret that she had not been brave enough to pursue her dreams.

"I chose my career because my parents wanted me to and it would be well respected in our community. But I can't help but think about what things would be like if I had been brave enough to stand up for my dreams. I wish I had at least tried," she said with tears in her eyes.

As her breathing worsened over the next day, she eventually needed to be intubated and put on a ventilator. She was transferred to the ICU at that time where she was closely monitored for the next two weeks.

Against all odds, she began to slowly recover. The ventilator settings were slowly weaned down until, finally, she was extubated. She was transferred out of the ICU and recovered well.

I received an envelope in the mail six months later. Inside was a card expressing kindness and gratitude, detailing that her cancer was now no longer spreading. She described that while she still worked for the technology company, she had scaled back her role there and, on the side, had started contributing to a publication as a technology specialist reporter.

There was also an article attached, reporting on the supply chain crisis for semiconductors used in smartphones. "Nicole Lin, Technology Writer" was the byline.

Sorrow for not pursuing one's dream is a common regret that many patients express on their deathbeds. On the other hand, throughout the whole pandemic, I never encountered a patient who regretted pursuing their dreams, even if their endeavors had ended in what some would consider failure.

John McDonald was a postman. He enjoyed his job in the way that many with a general positive attitude do, so much so that even at age seventy-six, he still had not retired. After a while, he got to know many of the families on his route and saw children grow up, some of whom would eventually buy homes down the block, also on his route.

He had always dreamed of being a painter, however.

"That is my true passion. When that starts taking off, then I'll retire," he told me with a chuckle when I first met him in the urgent care.

John loved painting and was always in some phase of painting a new portrait. He enjoyed entering his work into local art exhibits and competitions.

"See that painting of the farmhouse down the hallway? I donated that to the hospital back when they were first opening this wing up!" he said with glee as he was wheeled to his room.

Mr. McDonald's medical history was similar to Mrs. Lin's. Both of them had cancer (prostate in Mr. McDonald's case, breast in Mrs. Lin's), and both of them were severely immunocompromised and susceptible to COVID due to the cancer and chemotherapy they were undergoing.

Their hospital courses were similar as well. Mr. McDonald required increasing levels of oxygen support until, eventually, the highest level of HFNC was not enough. Soon, he needed to be intubated and transferred to the ICU.

But Mr. McDonald did not have any regrets about his choices.

"Back when I was in my twenties, I tried to make it as a painter alone. Unfortunately, that did not pan out. But I feel lucky that I am able to live a life where I can continue to paint when I'm not delivering. I do not regret trying to make it as an artist. This way, I'll never wonder, 'What if?' I own my own choices," he shared with me once when I rounded on his room.

Sadly, John McDonald did not have the same outcome as Nicole Lin. His condition continued to worsen, and he passed away. His daughter, Kelly, invited me to his funeral. It was a beautiful event where they displayed some of his favorite works of art.

Kelly gave me a large rectangular package as I said my goodbyes to her.

"Before the ventilator, he told me he wanted you to have this if he died."

The package contained a stunning painting of a hospital ward in the 1980s, complete with vintage hospital cots and stethoscopes.

Fulfillment at the end of one's life comes more from satisfaction with the decisions one makes, rather than the outcomes. Many regret not pursuing their dreams, but nobody regrets chasing their dreams and failing. So it is truly odd that many live their lives fearing this failure and living "safely."

When we follow our dreams, we learn who we really are. Chasing your dreams will drive you to identify what your life's work is. Belgian American poet May Sarton wrote, "We have to dare to be ourselves, however frightening or strange that self may prove to be."[80]

Pursuing our dreams is an imperative journey of self-discovery. How can we know ourselves if we do not even dare set down the path we desire? Mankind has always known that the passage of introspection is done by following your own heart. Legends say the words "Know Thyself" were carved into stone at the entrance to Apollo's temple at Delphi in Greece. And regardless of the risks, finding oneself is, most likely, worth it, regardless of if there is some financial or career incentive to chasing your dreams.

And yet, it is often the case that we find ourselves sacrificing our own dreams to help our bosses or some faceless megacorporation pursue their dreams. Of course, very few among us are lucky enough to have our dream jobs. But if you are young (feel free to define a specific age range yourself), then the current job you have of helping bosses realize their dreams will probably still be there for you, even if your journey requires you to leave this job to take a chance. However, I suspect many of us can get a start on our dreams even before we even consider leaving our "safety job."

Classic American actor John Barrymore said, "A man is not old until regrets take the place of dreams."[81] Few people are able to make it to death's door to have the realization that they regret not following their dreams, and then get a second lease on life like Nicole did. A conservative decision to put our dreams on the sideline may appear cautious now, but be warned that the same decision may appear foolish on your deathbed. Following *someone else's dreams* in your own life is even more absurd.

Be bold and have the courage to follow your dreams. Do not let fear of failure or disappointment resign you to a destiny of regret. We owe it to ourselves to make sure we follow our own dreams so we can own the end and lead a fulfilled life. You cannot control your death, but you can certainly live on your own terms.

Chapter 14

Be as water is.

Scripps Green Hospital, the historic hospital in La Jolla, where I served during the beginning of the COVID pandemic, is unique among health-care centers in that it is located right on the beach next to the Torrey Pines Golf Course and a vacation resort. In fact, as I walk from the parking garage to the wards, I can see the beach. The serene melody of the waves crashing against the sand contrasts with the cacophony of alarms that awaits me on the hospital floor.

Watching the golden sunset on the Pacific Ocean at the end of every shift is the perfect way to end each workday. As COVID cases in Southern California began to rise, my favorite view was obstructed by the unsightly presence of a large white tent that was erected next to the hospital to accommodate the influx of COVID testing. The laughter of families playing at the beach was replaced with the sound of the vacuum motor sealing the air pressure of COVID rooms, along with the sirens of ambulances bringing in a steady influx of patients.

Generally, I absolutely love living near the ocean. One hike on the Torrey Pines trails overlooking the oceanside cliff, and I knew I wanted to live in San Diego. The dance of the ocean's tide, the distinct saltiness it sprays into your nose, and the rich sapphire color extending into the horizon fills me with a sense of calmness and freedom. Perhaps that's why Ju Lao's philosophy of water resonated so well with me.

Ju Lao was born in California just one year after her parents immigrated from Taiwan. Her father was a computer scientist who imparted upon her the value of a good education, organized thinking, and hard work. Her mother was a *daoshi*, a Taoist priest who imparted upon her the value of spirituality, balance, and flexibility.

When she was born, Ju Lao's pediatricians noticed that she would turn blue when crying. It turned out that she had a congenital heart condition called "tetralogy of Fallot," which actually refers to four structural abnormalities taking place at once when a baby's heart does not form correctly.

The cardiovascular system is akin to a finely tuned car engine. It is an intricate system of pumps, tubes, and valves that requires careful structure and maintenance so that the pressure and flow remain in the appropriate range. In tetralogy of Fallot, there is a series of defects in the structure of the pump, which leads to incorrect flow. Specifically, there is 1) a hole in between the two big chambers of the heart, 2) severe narrowing of the pulmonary valve, 3) severe enlargement of the aortic valve, and lastly 4) a thickening of the musculature of the right lower chamber. This is a critical condition, as it causes the blood that is flowing to the body to be inadequately oxygenated.

Just as engine failure requires a mechanic to physically repair or replace the engine, treatment of tetralogy of Fallot is surgical repair of the heart. This is not an uncommon surgery, as according to the CDC, one in every 2,518 babies born in the United States each year are born with tetralogy of Fallot and require this surgery. Ju Lao successfully underwent the surgery with a fairly uncomplicated post-op course.

Growing up, Ju Lao followed in the footsteps of both of her parents. Her mother taught her Taoist philosophy and mindfulness. Their family was actively involved in the Taoist temple, which was located just a five-minute walk from their Chinatown apartment. After high school, she attended California Polytechnic State University to study computer science, inspired by her father, and she eventually went on to work at one of the world's major semiconductor companies.

Over the next two decades, she followed up regularly with her cardiologist to ensure that her heart continued to function well. In an appointment a month before I met her, her cardiologist noted that her right ventricle (lower chamber of the heart) was enlarging, which may require replacement of the pulmonary valve to ensure the flow of blood through the heart remained smooth.

When I met Ju Lao in the emergency room, she described that this morning, she had started feeling feverish with difficulty breathing with some swelling in her legs as well. Her cardiologist had warned her that if she ever experienced symptoms similar to these, she should come to the hospital immediately. She had originally been scheduled to go on an important business trip to Taiwan a week from now and asked if that would still be possible. I replied that although our hope was that she would be able to be discharged from the hospital by then, we would take it day by day.

She tested positive for COVID. Unfortunately, the infection had caused her cardiac condition to be further exacerbated, resulting in blood being backed up behind the heart and the heart beating in an atypical pattern (aka arrhythmia), known as "atrial flutter." She was admitted to the hospital so her heart rhythm and blood volume could be stabilized.

Physicians typically first round on their patients early in the morning between 6 and 7 a.m. so that they can make sure they've checked in on everyone before the new patients start rolling in. Every patient we see at this time is usually still sleeping. Ju Lao, however, was always already up. She would be seated cross-legged on her bed, facing the sunrise with her eyes closed and hands in a meditative pose.

As we worked with our cardiology colleagues to figure out the best plan for Ju Lao, it became clear that she would require surgery to replace the pulmonary valve of the heart, as it was currently preventing the proper flow of blood through the heart. This would mean that she would need to stay in the hospital a few more days and take careful rest even after leaving the hospital. No international business trips for the next month or so.

When I told her this, Ju Lao gave me a simple nod. I was taken aback at the calm reaction at not just having to cancel a very important business trip, but also learning that she would be having major cardiac surgery. She noticed my reaction and smiled at me.

"In life, we must be as water is. Water is resilient to the changing nature of life. When you put water in a cup, it changes its form so that it is now the shape of the cup." She held up a plastic cup as she spoke. "When it is part of the ocean, it waves. When it is hot, it evaporates. When it is cold, it becomes frozen. This is water's strength, as it is flexible and therefore resilient to changing circumstances. When something is brittle and dry, it will break under even small pressure. This is true even for the human mind. Even the hardest rock is conquered by the soft water over time."

When Ju Lao spoke, the whole room had an air of tranquility. Her voice evaporated any tension in the room. The sunlight shone on her face as she continued.

"Just like water in a river, you must flow smoothly, adapting your course to the changing nature of life. This is a fact of life so obvious, it is even apparent in my own heart! You must allow smooth flow, as turbulence and distress lead to a lack of balance and harmony."

Ju Lao successfully underwent the surgery the next week and recovered well. We still keep in touch, and she emails me links to Taoist books and poems.

She has had extensive training into mindfulness through growing up in an environment enriched with Taoist philosophy, but the theme of flexibility she taught me is something I have observed in many patients who are able to close the final chapter of their lives with contentedness and dignity. Patients who are at peace in their deaths are adept at adjusting to changing situations. Patients who are rigid in their thinking and unable to deviate from it find their mortality, especially if unexpected, to be a source of extreme stress.

Ju Lao is not the only patient of mine to use the metaphor of water or a river. I have had patients of different faith traditions share with me the importance of water in their spiritual traditions.

A Hindu patient of mine shared with me a narration from the Upanishads where water represents purity and authenticity in one's thinking: "As pure water poured into pure remains unchanged, so is the Self of the discerning sage."[82] The purity of water is a metaphor for ensuring that one's mindset remains uncontaminated by hate or fear.

This notion of purity with water is reflected in Christian traditions as well. The Bible states, "I will sprinkle clean water on you, and you shall be clean from all your uncleannesses, and from all your idols I will cleanse you."[83]

Baptism, a ritual of purity and rebirth in many Christian traditions, is done by sprinkling or pouring water on the individual's head.

In Islam, water is part of a ritual known as *wudu* to purify oneself before prayer and meditation. In ancient Islamic scripture, water is also used as a metaphor for nourishment. It is described as the source of life, as God "made from water every living thing."[84] It is used as a metaphor for the nourishment human beings must provide to those around them.

Being like water is a universal spiritual message that unites many traditions. The world's major spiritual traditions all seem to have sacred sites centered around water, such as the Zamzam in Islam, Lourdes in Roman Catholicism, and Ganges in Hinduism. There is a viral Bruce Lee interview clip where he describes this exact point.[85] The reverence humankind has for water goes back as far as history is recorded. Bodies of water held sacred significance in ancient Egyptian, Greek, and Roman societies.[86] This adoration of water continues today, as hotel rooms with views of water or water features are priced higher than those without, and real estate with close proximity to water is more expensive than others.

Evolving research in neuroscience and psychology suggests that water is something to which we are hardwired to respond. In an intriguing study where psychologists asked participants to recall their favorite childhood memories, they found that a significant contributor to whether a memory was positive or an experience was fulfilling was whether there was a body of water present.[87] Neuroscientists have found that when looking at urban settings or those without natural water, there is activation of the amygdala, which is the fear center of the brain. However, when looking at settings with natural bodies of water, this area does not light up and rather the areas associated with calmness and self-reflection are active.[88] Evolutionarily speaking, our ancestors who were near bodies of water were more likely to survive than those who were not, so it makes sense that the importance of water is infixed in our biology.

Even more significantly, water has been shown to create a meditative state. Studies have shown being near water makes us happier, healthier, and calmer.[89] Being near or even thinking and reflecting on peaceful scenes with bodies of water can allow our minds to enter a mindful condition. Gurus in mindfulness from various traditions and practices across the world will reflect upon water, often in a natural setting, to help them achieve the tranquility needed to attain transcendence. And environmental design researchers have even found that putting up posters with natural settings containing some body of water reduces anger and stress at the workplace.[90]

My own patients express similar sentiments. I have many patients in my clinic with arthritis, joint pain, or muscle pain. For many of them, I prescribe a specific type of physical therapy called aquatic therapy. These exercises take elements of gentle movements of tai chi while also incorporating modern elements of Watsu physical therapy. Aquatic therapy is designed to help patients strengthen their muscles and improve their range of motion in a manner that is non-weight-bearing. The support of the water allows patients to engage in exercises they may otherwise not be able to do with their physical therapist. My patients have reported that aquatic therapy helped them loosen their muscles, decrease muscle spasms, and regain functional activity. I cared for a patient with severe leg swelling due to edema who had improvement in their swelling using aquatic therapy. I suspect that the compression from the water pressure allowed for improved functioning of their lymphatic system thereby reducing their swelling.

The patients I refer for aquatic therapy also recount that, to their surprise, they noticed a change in their mental health as well. A patient recalled that, "While doing the exercises in the water, I felt like I was meditating. Just like my body felt weightless in the water, my mind also feels like there's been a big weight lifted off it."

Mental health researchers have found that aquatic therapy, in addition to the typical physical benefits of physical therapy, fosters a sense of wellness and balance in everyday life.[91]

The world's spiritual traditions use water to guide us on purifying our mindset and imparting upon both strength and flexibility, while neuroscience shows us that water activates the parts of our brain associated with meditation and mindfulness. It is unmistakable that water holds a great significance to allow us to enter the psyche needed to live a fulfilled life.

Water is flexible, but strong. Life, by its very nature, is ever-changing. Circumstances are ever-evolving and rarely expected. As someone who started his career in medicine right before a global pandemic, I can attest to this. But just like water, we must adapt to what life sends our way with flexibility and softness, as rigidity will make us fragile. As Lao Tzu says, "Water is fluid, soft, and yielding. But water will wear away rock, which is rigid and cannot yield. As a rule, whatever is fluid, soft, and yielding will overcome whatever is rigid and hard. This is another paradox: what is soft is strong."[92]

Water nourishes those around it. Life around water flourishes with its presence. It teaches us to be a force of growth in this world. As Suzy Kassem wrote in her poem "Mother is Water," "You are the fountain/ That nourished my growth,/And from your chalice—/Gave me life."[93]

Water is pure and teaches us not to let our mentality become contaminated. We should refuse to let the agendas and expectations of others influence our own happiness.

Water reminds us of our common humanity. Japanese writer Ryunosuke Satoro wrote, "Individually, we are one drop. Together, we are an ocean."[94]

As the COVID pandemic comes under control and a sense of normalcy begins to return to the hospital, the drab white COVID-testing tent is cleared, bringing back my favorite view of the Pacific

Ocean from Scripps Green Hospital. And as I gaze into the beautiful ocean sunset after every shift, I am reminded how being as water—through living a life of flexibility with strength, pure mindedness, and positive nourishment—is paramount to a fulfilling life.

Chapter 15

Break the cycle to open a closed mind.

ode Blue Alert. Room 692. The hospital PA system blared the alert, interspersed with ringing alarms, waking me up with a start after I had lain on the stiff cot for a mere five minutes. I rushed out of the call room to respond to the code. It had been wishful thinking to hope for an hour of shut-eye in the middle of the night.

During residency, internal medicine doctors typically spend a few months every year on the critical care team that cares for the sickest patients in the hospital, such as those in the ICU. It's a service that constantly keeps you on your toes with complex physiology involving the interplay of multiple diseases affecting several organs as you carefully titrate settings on ventilators and ECMO (heart-lung bypass) machines. The toughest part of the service as a resident physician are the twenty-eight-hour shifts, during which you stay in house overnight after your day shift to monitor the patients and respond to any emergencies.

I ran up the stairs to get to the sixth floor. That floor is the gastroenterology and hepatology ward; when you're on the critical care service, you respond to every Code Blue in the hospital whether the patient is on your list, just in case ACLS needs to be performed.

"Doctor, the patient is Justin Jones, an eighty-six-year-old male with cirrhosis here with spontaneous bacterial peritonitis and COVID-19," said Kelly, the patient's nurse, as I entered the room. "We came in and he was unresponsive. No pulse. Patient is full code."

I stood at the foot of the bed while the response team wheeled the code cart into the room.

"Continue compressions. Make sure we have IV access, and put on pads for rhythm analysis and shocks if needed," I said while looking over the patient's labs to figure out what the cause of his sudden crash was.

Kelly removed Mr. Jones's hospital gown so that the pads could be applied. There was a pause that followed as the bustle of the code was interrupted by a brief moment of hesitation. I looked to see what the cause was.

On Mr. Jones's chest was a tattoo of a red and black Nazi swastika. It was surrounded by a tattoo of a serpent baring its fangs and the words "Blood and Soil."

Time seemed to stand still, and the room suddenly felt cold. We all avoided looking at the vile symbol as if there were a hurtful glare emanating from it. The pause lasted a split second before everyone went back to compressions and resuscitations. *We're all professionals here.* It was not the first time any of us had cared for a patient who may not reflect our values, and it would not be the last.

Within two minutes, the monitor was up and running, showing that the cause of the patient's unresponsiveness was a critical heart rhythm called ventricular tachycardia.

"Push one milligram epinephrine and start charging to two hundred joules."

The defibrillator started humming, and it charged with electricity.

"Clear!"

Once I saw that everyone was safely clear of the patient, I administered the shock.

"We have a pulse!" Kelly exclaimed with relief.

Mr. Jones was transferred to the ICU after the code. He did not immediately regain consciousness and remained on the ventilator. Over the next twenty-four hours, we began a process known as targeted temperature management, in which ice-cold IV fluids were infused into Mr. Jones's body to lower his body temperature. This was done to prevent brain and tissue injury and preserve his overall function as his body recovered. As the days progressed, Justin Jones recovered against all odds and was even able to have the breathing tube removed.

I went to his room later that week to see how he was recuperating. He was awake when I entered the room. A blue hospital gown covered the symbol of hate I knew existed underneath. I was unsure of how he would react to seeing me, as I am quite obviously a person of color.

"I hear you're the one who saved me!" he croaked in a quiet voice. It is common for patients who have recently had a breathing tube removed to take some time before their vocal chords fully recover.

"It was a team effort. I'm glad you're doing better," I smiled pleasantly and took a seat next to his bed.

"I'm surprised you bothered doing CPR after seeing the tattoo on my chest," he said in a joking manner.

I froze, unsure how to respond to the sudden addressing of the elephant in the room.

He sensed it, but he was clearly accustomed to this reaction.

"I am not the same man I was when I got that tattoo," he continued. "I was in a very dark time in my life. I made many mistakes."

"What helped you come out of the darkness?" I asked.

"I got a new job, and my boss there was Black. Finest man I ever met. He showed everyone he met such kindness. When my father died, he was the only one who was there for me, providing me with emotional and practical support, while my white supremacist friends had abandoned me. That's when it simply clicked for me. I had been brainwashed and had never even taken a moment to critically think about the beliefs I held."

He opened his wallet and handed me a business card with his email.

"After that realization, I've dedicated my life to helping others see the light. You see, what happens to people is they get stuck in an echo chamber. This used to be in social groups but with the young kids I'm seeing now, it's with the internet. And they get stuck in a feedback cycle of only seeing information supporting their backwards beliefs, which

in turn makes their beliefs stronger and reinforces the echo chamber."
He had drawn a circle of arrows on the card as he was talking. "You
have to break the cycle in your own mind that is preventing you from
critically thinking, and then help others do so.

"Racist people hold their beliefs because their minds have been
closed due to this feedback loop acting continuously. Oftentimes
they are on the fringes of society, and their hate groups are the only
community they have. That's how it was for me. I break this cycle by
showing people they can belong in a diverse society."

He continued: "When you meet someone who has these crazy
views, it can be tempting to either ignore them or argue with them.
Neither of these approaches will work. What I have found is that you
must make them feel like they belong in a group outside the fringe one.
This will disrupt their echo chamber—but also, when they are exposed
to a peer group that is able to provide social support while not holding
the racist beliefs, they will be able to think critically about things they
were not able to previously. You must learn their perspective so they
can learn the perspective of others. The only way to fight hate is with
love, of course!"

By now, a feeling of shame began filling up my heart. I felt terrible
for having judged him based on the tattoo, particularly when he was
such an advocate. (In my defense however, there is a limited set of
conclusions one can come to when seeing a neo-Nazi tattoo!)

"Break the cycle to open a closed mind!" Mr. Jones exclaimed with
a fist pump.

The approach Justin Jones used to fight racism has been coined
"calling in" (rather than "calling out") by scholar and social justice
activist Loretta J. Ross. She teaches other activists that the common
occurrence of calling out, colloquially referred to as "canceling,"
may hold a place in holding the powerful accountable, but it is not a
productive method of fighting for justice among our peers. She notes,
"A call out isn't an invitation for growth; it's the expectation that
you've already grown."

Rather than reacting with anger or hate, it is better to remain calm and simply ask them to better explain their perspective. This approach allows you to get to know their thoughts and promotes a conversation so they can get to know other perspectives. In her vast experience as a social justice advocate, she has found that this is the way to change the minds of those with hate or prejudice in their hearts.[95]

I stopped by Mr. Jones's room frequently, as I really enjoyed our conversations and learned from his passion for finding the best in people. Sadly, his condition took a turn for the worse. Due to his liver disease, his body was already quite weak and had very little reserve to fight the COVID infection. His chest had been significantly damaged during the code the previous week, and broken ribs had injured his lungs. His breathing began to quickly worsen, and both his liver and kidneys began to fail.

After the experience of going through CPR, Mr. Jones had decided he would like to change his code status to not undergo heroic measures in case he should pass away. We discussed that with his current health, it was very unlikely that he would survive again, and if he did, would likely have very limited cognitive function.

"I am ready to die if that is what God has planned for me," he told me. "I can look back at my life with pride. Yes, I have made mistakes. But I have lived a life of redemption to help those who are in the darkness like I was."

Approximately a week later, Justin Jones died comfortably in his sleep. He was surrounded by family and friends who told me he died in peace.

Patients who hold prejudice in their hearts typically express profound regret and shame at their beliefs as they die. The closed-mindedness Mr. Jones taught me about is shattered open with the forced perspective induced by mortality. These patients are never at peace when they die.

Psychologists have proven that none of us are born racist or with hate. After all, there is no such thing as a racist baby.[96] Rather, hatred and prejudice are fostered by intrinsic issues in our society. Professors

Steven Roberts and Michael Rizzo, experts studying the psychological bases of racism and how to dismantle them, describe that racism is "triggered by factions, hardened by segregation, emboldened by hierarchy, legislated by power, legitimized by media, and overlooked by passivism."[97] It forms communities that in turn self-reinforce these ideas of hatred. The internet has further exacerbated this, as these communities can remain insulated from other perspectives and become even more extreme without any moderating voices or diversity in membership.[98] Attacking or directly attempting to call out individuals is important, but on a personal level, as Mr. Jones notes, the way to change their hearts is to expose them to more diverse points of view.

Justin Jones is not the only patient I've cared for over the course of the pandemic who has described how they once lived with some form of prejudice in their heart and were able to break the cycle and then be an ally. These patients, particularly the ones who worked to redeem themselves by actively being allies through supporting social justice organizations and voting accordingly, typically felt a great deal of pride at the end of their lives.

Justin Jones's experience tells us that firstly, fulfillment at the end of one's life can still be obtained if one works to redeem oneself. And secondly, opening one's mind in life to think critically about one's beliefs through being socially engaged with diverse arrays of individuals will improve one's perspective during life and lead to a greater meaning in both life and death.

Chapter 16

Be a good friend.

Summer in Hanover, New Hampshire, is muggy and sticky. The thick air hit me like a wall when I stepped out onto the campus from our family minivan for the first time. Born and raised in Northern California, I was used to a dry heat in the summer. When my parents helped me move in the beginning of freshman year at Dartmouth all those years ago, in addition to getting used to living alone for the first time in my eighteen years, I also had to adapt to far greater variance in weather than I had previously encountered. When my parents dropped me off on the historic Green, almost on cue, a flash summer thunderstorm soaked me as I walked to my dorm, conveniently masking my tears as I looked back at my parents driving away.

Luckily the college packs the first two weeks with a busy orientation schedule to ensure we don't have time to be homesick. The faculty give the newly minted freshmen a crash course on the basics of humanities as well as do placement tests to ensure everyone is starting with the right liberal arts coursework. One of the general courses we took covered the basics of the philosophy of classical antiquity. We were assigned reading from a mountain of sources, most of which I cannot even recall the title of, let alone the theses, but I remember my favorite excerpts were from Nicomachean Ethics for our lecture on Aristotle. Our professor told us that in his work detailing the successful human life, the singular topic most frequently emphasized by Aristotle was *friendship,* remarking that "without friends, no one would choose to live, though he has all other goods."[99]

Aristotle notes that simply being with others is not enough, that "it is better to spend his days with friends and good men than with strangers or any chance persons. Therefore, the happy man needs friends."[100]

Our professor then concluded the lecture series by telling us that perhaps one of the most valuable takeaways from our experiences in college would be lifelong friendships. Degrees and knowledge would certainly allow us to achieve career success, but our friendships would contribute equally, if not greater, to our happiness. Therefore, the wise among us would be careful in who we chose as our friends and be devoted friends to those we admitted into this circle.

This would certainly prove true, as I have been lucky to have met lifelong, ardent friends during my time in college. Although I'm sure I have not always done a perfect job, I have strived to be a steadfast friend to them, just as they have been to me. I have been reminded of this quality during the pandemic, where dedicated friendships have been a recurrent theme of those who have lived fulfilled lives.

Esther Barnes was a seventy-nine-year-old lady with a folksy, slow drawl that would make your heart melt. She spoke with a gentleness that somehow made you feel warm whenever you spoke to her. She was sitting in the patient chair, wearing a burgundy shawl with matching earrings and shoes when I first met her.

She had only been able to get the initial dose of the COVID-19 vaccination. Unfortunately, after the first dose, she had suffered from a rare but severe allergic reaction, which made her ineligible for the second dose and booster.

The hardest part of the pandemic for Esther thus far had been having to social distance from her friends. She loved seeing all of her friends at the bridge club, volunteering at the local animal shelter, or eating out at restaurants with her grandkids. With the social distancing guidelines, she had been unable to do her favorite activities.

Luckily, one of her grandkids had helped her set up a tablet computer so that she could video chat with her friends and family regularly. She was able to play online bridge, Bingo, and chess with her friends.

"Technology is incredible these days!" she exclaimed when describing it to me.

Despite all of her precautions, she unfortunately had begun having trouble breathing the previous week. When her condition did not get better after a few days, she decided to come to the hospital, where she was diagnosed with COVID-19.

Mrs. Barnes was working very hard to breathe and was having difficulty maintaining her oxygen levels, so we decided to admit her to the hospital so we could start therapeutics to treat the infection and keep a close eye on her breathing.

Over the next couple days, the respiratory therapy team administered the nebulized medications, but Mrs. Barnes's breathing did not improve. We continued to treat her, but her breathing worsened every day. When I went to her room the next morning, she looked breathless, but she also seemed quite down psychologically.

"I miss talking to my family and friends, doc. It has been so lonely. I'm sure they are quite worried about me too." She turned to look out the window, took a deep breath through the nasal cannula, and turned back to me with tears in her eyes and a soft smile on her face.

"I have been so lucky in life to have the friends I've had. They have given me love whenever I have needed it and been there for me in both joy and sorrow. Friendships have given my life meaning and happiness. I do not know how much longer I have left, or if I will survive this hospitalization, and I really wish I could see my friends and family," she said as she tenderly held my hand.

One of the most difficult aspects of patient care during the pandemic has been the strict visitation policy. Obviously due to the highly infectious nature of COVID, we had to limit the visitors to protect both the patients and potential visitors. This has been very difficult for both patients and their loved ones. COVID-19 is already a very scary illness. Not being able to visit a loved one in the hospital exponentially increases the fear and uncertainty for the family.

Our patients' isolation from their families has taken away an invaluable component of their recoveries. I have found that particularly for older patients, having a family member or close friend at the bedside helps the patient overcome their illness and do well overall in the hospital. Elderly patients are particularly susceptible to delirium in the hospital, a phenomenon colloquially referred to as "sundowning." The most effective way to both treat and prevent this condition is with reorientation by a familiar face, such as a family member or loved one.

In the pandemic surges, when visitation was limited, we were able to get a tablet and webcam for most of the patient rooms so they could video chat with their family. Of course, this is no substitute to having loved ones in the room physically, but it served as an adequate stopgap during the pandemic until each surge resolved.

I arranged to have one of these tablets set up in Mrs. Barnes's room so she could see her friends and grandchildren. The next time I rounded on her room, she was enthusiastically talking to a group through video chat. Whenever I saw her from then on, it seemed like she was introducing me to someone on the screen.

As I entered the room, she waved me over and introduced me to her friends Kathy and Diane. The three women had known each other for over forty years, having met at a volunteering session for Habitat for Humanity where they connected over a shared interest of reading and became best friends. Later that afternoon, when I went to her room to check on her, Esther introduced me to Jeremy and Mira via video chat, whom she had regularly played bridge with for the past two decades. She knew pretty much everything about them, and she told me all about their grandchildren.

Over the next three days, I got to know the usuals I'd see on Esther's tablet. Hearing their conversations, the genuine concerns all her friends had about her health, and the love they all shared was heartwarming and always made me look forward to rounding on her room.

The next morning at about 4 a.m., I was woken up in the call room with the dreaded page: Code Blue, room 923.

"That's Esther Barnes's room!" I thought as I sprinted toward the room.

"Doctor, the patient's heart suddenly stopped beating approximately two minutes ago. We've begun CPR," the nurse told me as I walked in.

I looked at the heart monitor, which showed a fatal rhythm called ventricular tachycardia.

"Let's get ready to shock. Charge. Everyone is clear. Shock!"

I led the code for almost forty-five minutes, continuing CPR, running STAT labs/tests, giving IV medications, and shocking the heart. Unfortunately, despite all our best efforts, we were unable to bring her back.

I called time of death.

It turned out that due to COVID-19, she had developed a massive blood clot that had migrated to the lungs in the main blood vessel supplying the lungs, a condition called *pulmonary embolism*. Although most of the deaths we saw in COVID patients were due to a gradual progression in the infection, resulting in a deterioration in respiratory status, occasionally we'd see someone suddenly die due to a pulmonary embolism or fatal heart arrhythmia.

Esther Barnes's grandson reached out to me the next day to invite me to her funeral, which I was honored to attend. There, I got to meet many people in person whom I had previously only met through Esther's tablet at the hospital.

"Esther was a friend who brought meaning to our lives. She was genuinely interested in our sorrows and difficulties. She was someone who was reassuring," Kathy told me.

"She got us to laugh at ourselves. She helped those close to her understand themselves better. She listened to us, and because of our friendship, we got to build an understanding of our desires and fears," Mira added.

Meaningful friendship is a recurrent theme I've observed in those who feel fulfilled during the final chapter of their lives. Importantly, these friends are different from acquaintances who one may socialize with, or know as a product of proximity, such as work. Rather the friendships that we've seen provide meaning to patients when they face death are those with *substance*.

Many patients are generally very socially active, but, sadly, when they are in the final moments of their life, they are quite alone. They may have spent a considerable amount of their life worrying what others thought of them, but this is not the foundation of true friendship. On the other hand, some patients may not have a large quantity of friends, but they have strong bonds with the ones they do have. These patients are never alone on their deathbeds, as their friends make it a priority to be there for them.

Mrs. Barnes's friends eloquently expressed the qualities such friendships have: a genuine interest in all aspects of each other's lives that helps individuals get to know both each other and themselves.

Chapter 17

Be kind to yourself.

Samia Khan had such a sweet voice that the velvety sound alone was soothing in nature. She was ninety-four years old, though she looked like she was in her sixties. She exuded kindness and smiled at everyone who entered her room.

A consequential side effect of us having to wear multiple layers of PPE is that sometimes not being able to see each other's facial expressions can impact the empathetic aspect of patient care. However, it felt like Mrs. Khan's bright eyes pierced straight through the PPE face shield, and although I couldn't see it, I knew for sure she was smiling by the creases on the sides of her eyes and cheeks.

When I met her during the middle of the second surge of the COVID pandemic, she told me how she had begun having fevers, a wet cough, and trouble breathing. She had initially tried quarantining at home, but when her breathing began worsening, she came into the urgent care, where her health-care team found she had low oxygen levels. The team started her on oxygen support and admitted her into the hospital.

Being in the hospital can understandably be a frustrating experience for many patients. To a certain degree, your freedom is taken away, as your schedule for each day is decided by your health-care team. Things generally happen slowly in the hospital. And there's a formal process for every little action.

All of the staff in the hospital remarked upon how patient Mrs. Khan always was with everyone. No matter if it was a therapy team that was running late from responding to an emergency, or if an alarm in another room kept going off and waking her up, she never seemed to be bothered.

Sadly, her condition worsened over the next three days. Her breathing became more difficult, and her oxygen level continued to decrease to the point that she eventually needed to be transitioned to high-flow nasal cannula. Despite all this, Samia Khan always seemed to be calm, centered, and at peace.

When she came into the hospital, we had discussed code status with her.

"If I am to die, then let me die in peace and with grace. I have lived such a fruitful and gratifying life," she told me.

We documented her code status as DNR, as per her wishes.

I learned more and more about Mrs. Khan as the days passed and we treated her. She told me how she used to be an educator by profession. She specialized in special education, working with kids with special needs.

"Working with special needs children was an incredibly tough job. Back then, we knew much less about developmental sciences than we do now," she shared with me. "The main tool we had was kindness and compassion. I learned to treat these children with kindness, but I also learned to treat myself with kindness.

"When you have children, you'll realize that you'll make a lot of mistakes when caring for them. Just as you would be kind to your child if they were to come to you after making a mistake, I've learned that good parents are also kind to themselves."

That week in the hospital was a particularly tough one on the wards. The health-care system was under a great deal of stress as every hospital in the area was over capacity, and there was concern that we would be out of ventilators soon. Everyone on the health-care team felt tired, and the COVID numbers only seemed to increase every day.

Through it all, Mrs. Khan watched us from her patient room. Of course, she was our patient, and we were the caretakers, but she would oftentimes be the one providing *us* with emotional support and encouragement.

One morning when the team rounded on her room, she saw all of our exhausted faces. We began discussing her vital signs and lab values for the day, but she stopped us. Years of being a teacher had made her quite astute to the state of those around her.

"Listen, y'all must start being kinder to yourselves. I see you spending the whole day running from room to room. Pouring your hearts into caring for each person. Make sure you also take the time to care for yourself just like you care for your patients," she gently told us, making eye contact individually with the entire medical team.

"Oh, don't worry about us Mrs. Khan; it's our job to care for you!" I tried to interject.

Samia Khan began shaking her head immediately.

"Young man, if you treated your patients the same way I see some of y'all treat yourselves, then you'd be a terrible doctor! As a former special needs teacher, I know we can be crueler to ourselves than we are to even our worst enemies. Would you ever tell your patient 'You're not working hard enough and can't handle this disease!'? No, of course you would not. Similarly, as you all deal with this incredible challenge, you must be kind to yourselves. Or else you will be discouraged and burn out."

A team of psychologists at UT Austin led by Dr. Kristin Neff has studied the exact point Samia Khan was making to us. Professor Neff has found that this self-care quality is found in many successful, happy, and fulfilled individuals. She calls it "self-compassion." Self-compassion is defined as being kind and understanding toward oneself in instances of pain rather than being harshly self-critical, perceiving one's experiences as part of the larger human experience rather than seeing them as isolating, and holding painful thoughts and feelings in mindful awareness rather than overidentifying with them.[101] Dr. Neff's team of researchers found that self-compassion had a significant positive association with measures of happiness, optimism, positive affect, wisdom, personal initiative, curiosity and exploration, agreeableness, extroversion, and conscientiousness.[102]

Self-compassion is different from another concept you may be familiar with: self-esteem. Self-esteem has been in vogue over the past few decades, particularly in the field of education. When I was going through elementary school, fostering a child's self-esteem was considered a major goal for some teachers. Those of you who are millennials will likely have had a similar experience. Self-esteem is an overall judgment of one's self-worth.

As schools began attempting to incorporate self-esteem bolstering attributes in the 1980s and 1990s, they unintentionally prioritized feeling *good* over actual achievements. Stereotypically, teachers and coaches gave awards and good grades to all students even in the absence of real achievements ("participation trophies"). Although the research is mixed, some psychologists believe this may have bred an increase in narcissism. For example, psychologist Dr. Jean Twenge describes how young people she calls "Generation Me" are tolerant, confident, open-minded, and ambitious but also disengaged, narcissistic, distrustful, and anxious.[103]

Self-compassion is different from self-esteem in that it is not about judging oneself as blindly positive. Rather, Professor Kristin Neff explains that "self-compassion is a way of relating to ourselves kindly, embracing ourselves as we are, flaws and all."[104]

Samia Khan continued, "I taught many new teachers how to teach and care for children with autism. Working with our children can be a very difficult job and requires a lot of patience. The children we worked with would go into many tantrums throughout the day, screaming often and sometimes even physically striking the teachers.

"I found that the teachers would become discouraged and take these moments as failures and signs that they were not up to the task. Of course, they would never think that of their students and other teachers. But we're harsher on ourselves, and criticizing ourselves when we aren't accomplishing our goals shatters our motivation and drive.

We'll burn out. And then who will care for the children? Or in your case—the patients?"

Scientific research supports exactly what Mrs. Khan told us. Scientists have proven that when we self-criticize, we experience feelings of unworthiness, inferiority, failure, and guilt. A more effective approach is treating ourselves with care when confronted with inadequacies, failures, and painful situations. Studies have shown that self-criticism is destructive, while self-compassion is associated with healthy relationships, emotional well-being, and better outcomes.[105]

Mrs. Khan and Dr. Neff's philosophy of self-compassion was something quite foreign to me initially. The path to becoming a doctor—namely medical school and residency—similar to many other career training paths in life, fosters self-criticism. Most of us learn to berate ourselves when we don't live up to our own ambitions. And this works for a while, flogging us to do our best on the MCAT, USMLE exams, and every other hurdle they throw at us. I can speak to the path to my career, but the research suggests that this is a common quality many individuals experience, fostered by college, grad school, or apprenticeship training.[106]

Growth driven by self-criticism works only until it does not. The breaking point for many in health care was the COVID-19 pandemic, where this form of self-criticism resulted in depression.

I must admit, when I first heard about self-compassion, I was leery. Before I read the science behind it, I thought it sounded like a new-age, self-indulgent attitude, the kind of thing you'd hear baby boomers complain millennials are doing. But I saw my colleague resident physicians keep criticizing themselves with every COVID wave and nurses being overworked and subsequently burning out. Then I met Mrs. Khan, and I decided to try to instill self-compassion into our team culture to avert burnout.

While going through the pandemic, I worked to actively engage in self-compassion mindfulness exercises during our team rounds, particularly when a patient outcome didn't occur the way we'd hoped. We made sure to always keep in mind that, particularly with the pandemic, being in health care was difficult. We'd remind ourselves that there are many things that we as doctors cannot control. Sometimes you'll do everything right and things just won't turn out how you'd like them to.

Not everyone was as lucky as me. As the pandemic raged on, nurses, doctors, and other health-care workers faced a largely unprecedented amount of death on a daily basis—far more than their training had prepared them for. In fact, the American Psychiatric Association found that nearly half of all health-care workers reported serious psychiatric symptoms, including suicidal ideation, during the COVID-19 pandemic. [107]The nursing profession was particularly affected. There was significant turnover and shortage in registered nurses due to the pandemic. Granted, the mental health burden of the pandemic on health-care workers stems from serious systemic issues in the American health-care system that burden health-care providers. Nevertheless, I feel incredibly lucky to have met Samia Khan when I did so that she could instill the virtue of being kind to myself when times were darkest.

Although Mrs. Khan brought this concept of self-compassion to us explicitly, upon reflection, I realized that this was a common frame of mind that many of my patients had. Laila Ali, a heroic advocate for abuse survivors whom you will meet in a few chapters, had this mindset when she'd care for survivors facing absolutely deplorable situations. Bart Scully had this mindset when he faced constant rejection of his initial manuscript. Mary Roger had this mindset when dealing with her chronic illnesses.

My experience applying these lessons is in health care, but I'm sure that they are universal lessons that can be applied to any situation where one is experiencing defeat or loss.

I once cared for a patient who was elected to a position in local government. She had lost many elections before she finally won her seat. Even after winning, she struggled to pass her legislation. To make matters worse, she was criticized by local radio hosts, being a liberal in a conservative county.

When I asked her how she dealt with all the negativity, she told me, "I'm just kind to myself. I look at every defeat not as failure but rather, simply, as an opportunity to learn and try again. And I'm proud of myself for simply trying. If you don't treat yourself with compassion, how can you expect others to?"

As a physician, I meet a lot of EMTs, particularly when they bring in a transfer to the wards or a patient into the emergency department. As first responders, they see a lot of cases where, despite all their efforts, the patient will not make it, oftentimes before they can even come to the hospital. In fact, the survival rate of an out-of-hospital cardiac arrest is about 9 percent when there is an expert there to do CPR.[108]

"No matter what happens, I never take the burden of failure upon myself. I am kind to myself and always proud of myself as long as I can honestly say I did my best," an EMT buddy of mine shared with me.

Mental health experts have studied EMTs due to the high-stress nature of paramedics' jobs and the large amount of exposure to workplace trauma and PTSD. Experts found that actively engaging in self-compassion is protective for high-risk jobs, such as paramedics and firefighters, against mental health trauma.[109]

Samia Khan sadly passed away a few days later as the infection spread and her body could not keep up. The kindness and wisdom that she imparted on everyone who had the honor of meeting her while she was in the hospital will stay ingrained in our hearts forever. I am almost certain that had she not taught us about self-compassion, our team of doctors would have burned out during the pandemic.

The Neff research group has found that self-compassion has three major components. First is self-kindness. This refers to treating ourselves with the same empathy, gentleness, and compassion as we would treat a good friend. If one of our friends were going through a tough time, we would both emotionally support them as well as work with them to develop a plan. When dealing with ourselves, we oftentimes may do the latter, but do not positively support ourselves. Rather, we may revert to self-criticism, which can further exacerbate the problem.

The second component of self-compassion is knowledge of one's common humanity. A part of the shared human experience is imperfection. The normalization of making mistakes, both for others and especially ourselves, is critical to our happiness. Knowing and embracing our own flaws, as well as those of others, allows us to be kinder to ourselves and others. The norm, however, appears to be a sense of isolation from others when one falls or is going through hard times. Our reflex thinking is that it is unnatural to fail, have weaknesses, or go through adversity, triggering a reaction of "why me?" Of course, that is not the case at all. Suffering is part of our shared human experience, and self-compassion promotes a feeling of connectedness to others when experiencing suffering.[110]

Scientists have even proven that suffering is a part of our shared human experience, though human beings think they are more alone in their emotional difficulties than they really are.[111] We assume that we are the only ones making mistakes or suffering, and we then refuse to forgive ourselves. But everyone is going through the same thing—we just don't share it with each other. Of course, when we do, the compassionate among us reassure and forgive. But we must extend that same level of respect to ourselves.

The third component researchers found underlying self-compassion was mindfulness. Mindfulness provides us with the ability to be present in the moment, which underlies our internal validation of our suffering so that we can give ourselves compassion. Dr. Neff found that oftentimes, we are not aware of our own suffering. This is particularly the case when the result of the suffering is our own harsh self-criticism.[112]

The person we hang out with most is *ourselves*. We owe it to ourselves to treat ourselves with a certain amount of respect and deference. My patients have taught me that in order to have a life of self-fulfillment, you must have a mindset of self-compassion, especially when things get hard. Being overly critical may result in some productivity in the short run, but in the long run will result in a deterioration of this self-relationship, just as a friendship would deteriorate if you were constantly overly critical, no matter how well-intentioned.

Life is hard, unexpected, and short. My patients have taught me that in order to give it positivity, you must be kind to yourself.

Chapter 18

Don't weigh yourself down.

D r. Sofia Francisco was a patient I had known for years, as she would come to my clinic for regular checkups. As someone with both an MD and PhD, she was a very skilled researcher as well as clinician at the same institution, and everyone in the building found her to be exceptionally charismatic, hardworking, and kind.

She was ambitious, continuously writing grants and managing several major research labs while also taking on leadership positions and task forces. She would joke that she could not bear any empty slot in her calendar, so she always had to fill it with something productive.

Someone on the outside looking in would say that Dr. Francisco had an affinity for the finer things, as she would always be driving a new Mercedes-Benz and would upsize her home every few years. She always looked like she had stepped right out of an issue of *Vogue* magazine, wearing tailored designer clothing adorned with twinkling jewelry.

"I make it to spend it!" she would say with a laugh when showing us her latest purchase.

But as our friendship grew, Dr. Francisco confided in me that she did not feel as fulfilled as she thought she would have.

"It feels like I'm on a never-ending stairway to get to the next thing, but when I get to the next level, I don't feel any happier."

Dr. Francisco had a major epiphany when her world was turned upside down. She first noticed a lump in her breast. She thought it was most likely benign; she got it checked out just in case.

After undergoing several tests, including a biopsy and scans, she learned that the lump was breast cancer. However, fortunately, it was still in a relatively early stage. I promptly organized her follow-up with oncology so she could be started on hormone treatment and chemotherapy to treat the cancer, and she underwent a mastectomy to remove the cancer and at-risk breast tissue.

As I saw her in clinic appointments over the next few months, I observed Dr. Francisco make a slow and gradual recovery. The cancer treatment had severely weakened her body, but through her own strength and willpower, she was making it through with grace.

I noticed another change in her as well. Strangely, despite all the hardship she was going through, Dr. Francisco seemed *happier* and more *free*.

"Being diagnosed with breast cancer gave me a new perspective on life. After looking back on my life so far, I saw that I had spent so much of it trying to get things I *thought* would make me happy, at the expense of what I *knew* would provide me happiness and fulfillment," she excitedly explained to me.

She then spoke of how she had spent so much time working so that she could afford a new house, car, high-end furniture, etc. These luxuries, in turn, had increased her expenses, which then forced her to work even more to maintain the lifestyle. She hadn't realized it before, but she had entered into a cycle that ate up all of her free time.

When she was diagnosed with cancer, she thought of the happiest moments in her life, which consisted of times spent with family and friends and serving her community. She noted that the more advanced in her career she became, the less time she was able to spend on what brought her happiness.

At this insight, she began changing how she lived her life.

"First, I went through all of my *things,* and I sorted them into whether they brought me happiness or took away from it. This led to me downsizing my home and eliminating a lot of the clutter in my life.

"Second, I did the same thing with my time. I observed where my time was being spent and made the same categorization of whether or not those things made me happy. I then 'downsized' the commitments that were not contributing to my happiness and fulfillment."

She noted that these two things were mutually reinforcing. Because she had simplified her life, she had more free time, which she could spend doing what she loved.

Later that year, Dr. Francisco moved to the Midwest to be closer with her family. We kept in touch, and she would send me pictures of a community clinic that she was able to establish with her friends as well as blog posts from her travels around the world.

A year later, when the first COVID pandemic surge hit, I was saddened to hear that Dr. Francisco had gotten COVID while working as a frontline worker. Unfortunately, she did not survive the infection and passed away. Her family honored me by inviting me to her funeral, via video at that time to respect social distancing guidelines.

Her daughter, Lily, shared with me that on her deathbed, Dr. Francisco was very fulfilled and happy.

"Mom wanted me to tell you how grateful she was. She felt that both the cancer and the whole treatment was a blessing, as it gave her perspective on her life before it was too late, so that she could *live,*" Lily told me with tears in her eyes through the webcam.

Dr. Francisco's perspective is one that we observe in many patients who are fulfilled at their death. Specifically, we've noted how efficient allocation of one's life provides people with peace.

It's important to note that before this perspective shift, it's not as if Dr. Francisco was living outside of her means. She did not have an exorbitant, debt-fueled lifestyle. (Although, as a side note, I have found that those who do have debt-fueled, luxurious lifestyles inevitably regret it immensely when looking back at their lives.) Rather, it would be more accurate to describe her situation as "lifestyle creep," a phenomenon where one spends more money as they earn more money, getting used to higher levels of luxury and convenience as the new normal.

Dr. Francisco was not doing anything she couldn't afford, but her lifestyle was not affording her the freedom she desired in order to do what she *wanted*. Her life had been filled by both metaphorical and literal clutter that was weighing her down.

When she shed the factors in her life that were weighing her down but not contributing to her happiness—such as the exceptionally large home with the expensive mortgage, which had forced her to work overtime—then she found the freedom to do what brought her life meaning, such as establishing the community clinic and spending time with her loved ones.

Additionally, she did not resort to switching to a severely minimalist lifestyle. Dr. Francisco was very diligent and specific regarding what to remove from her life and what to keep. She sold the extra car she had because she noted that having another car came with a series of additional tasks, such as managing the maintenance, that did not provide her with the happiness she thought it would. However, she still made sure she always had a relatively new model of smartphone, as she found that the increased connectivity with her friends provided her with happiness. She still lived quite comfortably, though in a manner that optimized the allocation of both her resources and time to maximize her freedom.

Patients who feel fulfilled at their death have, largely speaking, structured their lives in a similar way to Dr. Francisco. They remove what is weighing them down in a manner that promotes a balanced lifestyle, so they can still live life and enjoy the experiences with the freedom to choose what experiences they engage in. On the other hand, patients who have spent their lives blindly chasing consumption oftentimes have expressed regret at doing so; they share that, upon reflection, *working more to get more* did not bring them any long-term happiness.

As George Carlin put it, "We buy shit we don't need, with money we don't have, to impress people we don't like."

This is an area of ongoing research in the field of psychology, so the literature on consumerism and minimalism is still underway. The research thus far, however, aligns with our experience with our patients. Studies on low-consumption lifestyles and behaviors have generally found that people who engage in such actions have higher levels of personal well-being.[113]

Chapter 19

Know that this too shall pass.

L aila Ali was known to the health-care workers and case managers in the hospital before she even walked through our doors as a patient. Many years ago, she came to this country as a refugee escaping religious persecution. She studied social work, eventually getting her master's degree. After graduating, she started working with a nonprofit organization that supports women who are survivors of domestic violence. Specifically, she and her colleagues from a variety of backgrounds worked to provide culturally competent aid to the survivors who were recent immigrants in order to best serve them. She had just turned eighty this past year and still remained active in the organization.

As physicians, we see many heart-wrenching cases of deplorable individuals abusing survivors, both physically as well as mentally. In fact, it is important as health-care workers to always keep our antennae up for abuse, as survivors may not have a safe space to discuss the abuse. We must, therefore, stay vigilant and look for subtle cues that may indicate abuse in order to get the patient to safety if needed. Nonprofit organizations, such as the one where Laila worked, play a very important role in supporting our patients through providing local support systems, advocates, and safety communities.

Laila came into urgent care during the beginning of the second surge of the pandemic. She had begun having difficulty breathing and decided to come in to get tested for COVID. Laila suffered from a lung disease—which had developed as a result of exposure to dangerous particles in her lungs when she was immigrating as a refugee—called interstitial lung disease. Because of this, her respiratory system was very stiff, fragile, and susceptible to infections. On top of this, a decade ago, she had battled lung cancer. Fortunately, the cancer had been in remission now for the past five years.

Her COVID test came back positive. As we monitored Laila closely in the urgent care, we saw that her oxygen levels were staying low and she required oxygen support via nasal cannula to maintain adequate levels. We decided to admit her to the hospital so we could keep a close eye on her breathing, as well as treat her with intravenous steroids so the inflammation in her lungs could be improved.

As has been standard of care during the pandemic, I clarified her code status when admitting her to the hospital so we knew what measures to take in case of an emergency where her heart stopped. Because of her frequent interactions with the health-care system, both personally and with her profession, she already knew the lingo and was able to answer as soon as I brought up the subject.

"Doc, I would not like any heroic measures done to my body if I die, and I do not want to be attached to a ventilator if my lungs fail. I know that because of my medical history, my chance of survival is very low, and even if I were to survive, I would be suffering through the remainder of my existence," she told me.

I nodded in understanding.

"I have lived a very blessed life thus far," she continued. "God delivered me from such a terrible circumstance, and I have had the honor of serving others who are going through the same. If death is what is next for me, then I have no regrets."

Over the course of the next day, Laila continued to have increased difficulty breathing. The respiratory therapy team worked diligently, treating her with nebulized medications to clear her airways, but unfortunately because of the chronic pulmonary disease, the infection spread rapidly.

I spent a lot of time in her room to assess the response of the therapies and closely monitor her respiratory status. During this time, Laila shared her life story with me. When migrating as a refugee, she went through unspeakable horrors. She shared with me the hardship of having her autonomy seized from her by horrible monsters. I still feel a lurch in the pit of my stomach as I recall the tragic story she shared. She then related how she had overcome such horrors with sheer willpower and strength, reclaimed her sovereignty, and made a better life for herself.

Her experience motivated her to help others do the same. She met individuals going through the same pits of hell she had navigated through years earlier, and she felt honored she could guide other survivors.

As I got to know her, I asked her what got her through those darkest moments, both in her life as well as with those she supported. I was curious, as during the pandemic surge when we were overrun with patients and experienced such a large amount of death, it felt like we were in a darkness. (Although of course my struggle pales in comparison to Laila's.)

"A kind Imam who looked out for us and helped me escape would always tell me to never forget that 'this too shall pass,'" Laila recalled. "He shared with us the scripture that says, 'Verily every hardship comes with ease.'

"Life is full of cycles, full of ups and downs. When times are darkest and you feel there is no hope, you must remember that even after the darkest night, the sun will rise. *This too shall pass.* Just keep walking and believing. Many before you have walked through darker tunnels and made it out the other side."

She then turned to me and added with a knowing look on her face, "You must remember this when times are brightest as well. Nothing lasts forever. When everything is working out your way, remember that *this too shall pass.* Cherish when times are good, and be mindful that they will not always be so."

Over the next five days, Laila's condition deteriorated. Her oxygen support needed to be increased to a high-flow nasal cannula, but eventually even this was not enough. The infection spread, and her other organs began to fail.

Up until her final moments, Laila appeared to be at peace, even during the last couple of days when she knew she would likely pass. She would get many phone calls and video chats from family and friends (recall that during COVID surges, visitors were limited). So many of the individuals she had helped throughout her lifetime wanted to now check in on her. As I would monitor her status during her critical state, I got to know her family and her close friends. Everyone I met said a variant of, "She's always been there for us, so now we want to be there for her."

Despite all our efforts, eventually her heart stopped, and I called time of death. Her family graciously invited me to Laila's funeral where I was able to meet many of those she had impacted.

Over the course of the pandemic, whenever things seemed dark, Laila's words would echo in my mind. *This too shall pass.* Countless times, they gave me the strength to make it through a difficult twenty-eight-hour shift.

I also remember her words when I feel on top of the world after saving a life or making a very difficult diagnosis. They remind me to cherish these moments and know that everything is transient in life.

I have observed this same sentiment of being cognizant of the transitory nature of highs and lows expressed by many patients at the end of their life as they reflect back on the ups and downs. Although not everyone is as eloquent as Laila, they express how knowing that calamity is often transitory has given them the willpower to get through it and has resulted in a gratifying life. When going through the ups and downs of life, they were mindful of the overall picture, so as to provide hope during the lows and foresight during the highs.

Moreover, many patients have expressed to me that when looking back on their lives, they wished they had not been so caught up in the cyclical ebb and flow. They spent their lives preoccupied with the trees, but being faced with their impending mortality forces a perspective shift of seeing the forest.

Many wish they could tell their younger selves that the difficulties they were going through would end soon, and to keep hope and be at peace. But of course, negative situations never seem that way when we are living through them.

New research confirms the positive effect of Laila's philosophy. In the field of psychology, the ability to have a "this too shall pass" perspective is known as "temporal distancing." A scientific review done by researchers at the University of California at Berkeley found that temporal distancing plays an important role in emotional coping with negative events, and that it does so by directing individuals' attention to the impermanent aspects of these events.[114]

Psychologists have found temporal distancing to be an effective attitude to adopt in many situations. For example, when studying students who were going through a stressful time, they found that having this perspective reminded them of the transience of the stressor and their reasons for pursuing a degree in their major.[115] A recent study done in Waterloo during the pandemic researched how this perspective could help individuals get through the stressful times of COVID. Researchers were interested in what exercises allowed participants to adopt the "this too shall pass" attitude. They found that taking a broader temporal perspective can be achieved by letter writing to your future self, and this practice resulted in regulating negative affect in a stressful present time.[116]

Laila, in her wisdom, did not wait for death to give her this perspective. She held it throughout her life, which was filled with more hardships than many of us can even imagine. This gave her the hope and strength needed to make it through as well as guide many others through desperate straits.

I have found that since actively instilling this mindset into my life, I have been able to keep hope. During the Omicron surge of COVID, our whole team would remember Laila's words when the hospital system was once again at more than full capacity. Although it was difficult, we had faith that it would pass.

And now that times (at least on the COVID front as of 2022) are a bit better, we cherish every moment, as we know that *this too shall pass*.

Chapter 20

Never skip breakfast.

"Doctors make the worst patients" is a running joke among health-care providers. We guide patients with the best advice and treatment we can provide, but oftentimes we will not follow our own instruction. This is especially prevalent for resident physicians, who typically work eighty hours per week. The long hours mean that resident doctors do not exercise as much as they probably should, and the stress of twenty-eight-hour calls means they usually resort to comfort foods rather than healthy, balanced, home-cooked meals as they're trained to recommend to their patients.

A cup of coffee and a bagel were jokingly known as the "breakfast of residents" as it is the typical meal at the morning report conference at academic hospitals across the country. (For the resident physicians who have the time to make it.) When on busy services, even this meager meal becomes a luxury.

Every morning at 7 a.m. when I entered Steve Costner's room on rounds, he would either be making his bed or eating breakfast. I'd take a few minutes to sit down with him as he ate to talk about how he was feeling. As I'd noticed his tray full of scrambled eggs, bacon, and hashbrowns, I'd think to myself that I was glad I couldn't smell the food through my N95 mask. Oftentimes, I find myself skipping breakfast in the mornings, and I'm sure that if I could smell my patients' breakfasts, my stomach would be growling to no end. Once Mr. Costner asked me if I'd had breakfast. When I replied that I hadn't, he actually chastised me.

"You can't skip the most important meal of the day! You ought to know better!" he playfully scolded.

He had come in a few days earlier after some abnormal lab tests during routine screening with his primary care physician. When he came into the emergency room, he was found to have a liver injury due to COVID-19. Since he was not able to maintain adequate oxygen levels due to the ongoing COVID infection, we decided to admit him to the hospital. He had a history of severe asthma and was at high risk for worsening of his respiratory status.

Mr. Costner, at age eighty-four, was a decorated researcher in physics. He had made many prominent discoveries and even published a few textbooks that I recall studying back in college.

I asked him how he was able to accomplish such an impressive body of work over his lifetime.

As he cut up his potatoes and eggs, he told me with a chuckle, "You know how I got this far in life? I never skip breakfast and always make my bed.

"If you get up in the morning and make your bed, you're starting out the day by already accomplishing something. Follow this up by eating a solid breakfast. If you begin each day by doing these two back-to-back tasks, you're already in the mindset of accomplishing things off your to-do list. You'll be inclined to continue this and keep accomplishing things throughout the day. Not to mention, you'll have an organized room and a full stomach to accomplish these things."

The COVID infection progressed, and Steve Costner's breathing worsened over the next couple of days. We discussed that because of his severe asthma and other chronic conditions, he was at high risk for severe worsening of the infection. Given the data on COVID-19 and his past medical history, there was a significant chance he would not make it if he were required to be intubated. When I discussed code status with him, he stated he wanted to be full code, even though his chances of survival would be low.

"I understand. If I leave this life because of this infection, I will be content. I have lived my life with discipline so that I have contributed a lot over the years. I am grateful for living my life like this, as it has allowed me to leave behind a legacy."

Generally speaking, there are several health benefits to eating a healthy breakfast every day (although of course one should note that different nutrition styles will work for different individuals, and eating unhealthy meals regularly will not be positive for your health, even if you *are* eating breakfast). Eating a *healthy* breakfast every day can help one maintain energy levels throughout the day, keeps a healthy level of metabolism, and can reduce snacking on unhealthy foods throughout the day.

But importantly, the regular discipline that Professor Costner described is a trait we have observed in many patients who are satisfied with their sense of accomplishment when they are near death.

Making one's bed and eating breakfast every morning are traits I have observed regularly in patients. And although they may seem like trivial practices, these daily habits likely represent an internal discipline and detail orientation that serves as the common denominator in these patients.

From a health standpoint, there is ongoing research on the power of developing daily habits and discipline, as instilling daily habits has been associated with both the prevention and treatment of chronic diseases, including coronary heart disease, diabetes, obesity, and cancer.[117] Morning routines may be more important than we realize, as research indicates disruptions in our morning routines can have ramifications on our stress level and productivity for the rest of the day.[118]

Admiral McRaven, retired United States Navy four-star admiral who served as commander of the United States Special Operations Command and chancellor of University of Texas university system, expressed a similar sentiment in a speech to graduates, stating, "If you want to change the world, start off by making your bed. If you make your bed every morning, you will have accomplished the first task of the day. It will give you a small sense of pride, and it will encourage you to do another task, and another, and another."[119]

Professor Costner's breathing continued to worsen. Three days after coming into the hospital, one early morning, I heard the dreaded "Rapid Response, room 789" on the overhead speaker. When I entered the room, I saw that his oxygen levels were quite low, and he needed to be intubated.

I gently explained to him that he would need to be intubated. He nodded in understanding and between labored breaths, expressed gratitude to the entire health-care team for caring for him.

Before we intubated him, he shared a private moment with his daughter and wife, filled with both laughter and tears, during which he told them how blessed he felt to have lived the life he had, and how gratified he was to have had the support of his family through everything.

"I'm nothing without them, doc. Without their love, I don't even think I'd have enough energy to make my bed."

We transferred Steve Costner to the ICU where we carefully monitored his respiratory status on the ventilator and treated with both IV steroids and nebulizer medications. Even with the odds stacked against him, he pulled through and eight days later, his lungs were strong enough that he could be extubated.

Two days after that, Mr. Costner was ready to be transferred out of the ICU and to the general wards, where I was able to resume taking care of him and monitoring his recovery as he got ready to be discharged from the hospital.

Our team had also progressed over this same time period. We all began making a point to wake up twenty minutes earlier in order to make sure we ate a full, balanced breakfast before coming into work. Admittedly, we were not able to accomplish this *every* day, but the effort was a start. And we found our energy levels were far better on the days where we were able to manage to do so. On the days when we weren't able to manage breakfast, we made sure to structure our mornings so that we at least made it to the morning report conference to eat the infamous "breakfast of residents."

I walked into Mr. Costner's room for morning rounds and found him conscious for the first time in eight days. He was sitting in the chair next to a fully-made bed, eating whole wheat toast with avocado.

"Good morning, Dr. Abbasi! I hope you didn't skip breakfast today!" he said to me with a big smile.

This time, I was ready with my answer.

Chapter 21

Ignite laughter.

Kristy Wharton had the kind of booming roar that filled up the whole hallway whenever she'd laugh. Her short, curly silver hair would bob up and down whenever she'd chortle. Her eyes always seemed bright, lighting up the whole room, and she had creases on the sides of her eyes and forehead from a lifetime of grinning.

Mrs. Wharton was no stranger to the hospital. She had been battling colon cancer, which had taken a significant toll on her health, and she had been in and out of the hospital for the past five years. It had been a difficult battle, as the chemotherapy had caused her to become quite weak. But luckily, the cancer had been identified relatively early during a screening colonoscopy and the main malignancy had been removed with surgery, and the small nodular spread treated with chemotherapy.

Throughout the whole ordeal, she had kept a very positive attitude. Even in the worst of it, she worked to maintain a happy state of mind. Her oncology physicians and nurses remarked upon how she always uplifted the mood of the entire clinic whenever she'd come in for an appointment.

As with many patients, Kristy Wharton first started experiencing a dry cough, which had progressed to difficulty breathing over the next few days, prompting her to come into the urgent care, where she was found to have COVID.

When I first met her in the urgent care room, I immediately noticed her brilliant smile when she greeted me—the kind of smile that instills joy and makes you smile as well.

I carefully examined her and noted that her breathing was using extra muscles—a physical exam finding called "accessory muscle use," signifying she was working harder than usual to breathe—and her oxygen level was borderline. After discussing with her, we decided to admit her to the hospital to watch her overnight and see if she needed to be monitored inpatient for longer.

Later that day, her initial lab work results came in. Her bilirubin and liver enzymes were elevated in a pattern that signified an obstruction in the biliary tract, which can be thought of as the pipe that connects the liver, gallbladder, and bowel. This, paired with her relatively unremarkable abdominal physical examination, is quite a morbid finding, as it can indicate a biliary or pancreatic cancer causing the obstruction.

Breaking a concerning lab finding that may indicate cancer to a patient is something that requires empathy and compassion when doing so, as you must communicate the result and likely plan with the patient, while also expressing emotional support and reminding them that they will not go through this process alone.

The PPE worn by doctors and nurses when caring for COVID patients consisted of an N95 mask, full-body gown, and protective face shield. As facial expression and touch can be such an important aspect of expressing empathy, it has provided an additional challenge for health-care providers to be able to provide the empathy and emotional support, while also using PPE to ensure a safe environment. There have even been studies showing that PPE limits nonverbal communication by masking providers' facial expressions and body language.[120]

During the pandemic, I tried to make sure that my communication remained empathetic by emphasizing compassionate language, since my patients may not be able to see my facial expression.

★★★

I gently told Mrs. Wharton the news about the lab results and that we would need to do additional imaging and potentially a biopsy over the next day to further evaluate what was causing the abnormalities and if it was cancer.

She told me she understood and gave me a soft smile with her eyes.

I swung by her room later that day to see how she was doing. I saw that she was video chatting with some friends, and although she still had sadness in her eyes, she was smiling and laughing.

When she saw me enter the room, she told me, "I always make sure my friends bring positive energy into my life. In life, I have been very careful and deliberate about who I become close with. I have found such an amazing group of friends who provide me with constant positive energy and support, and in turn, I do the same for them."

"How do you make sure they're the type of people who will bring positivity to your life?" I asked her, genuinely curious, as she was easily one of the most positive individuals I'd ever met.

"You see if they're the type of people who ignite laughter and happiness when times are darkest. During my last bout with cancer, I of course felt sad at first. But my friends were with me every step of the way. And when they saw that I was sad, they worked to make sure I was laughing," she answered, now with a big smile on her face.

Her friend, who was still on the tablet video chat, chimed in.

"Kristy, you've always done the same for us! You always make us smile and laugh. And when we need emotional support, you're always there for us. You're the one who taught us how to be forces of positivity for our friends!" she said.

Carefully and purposefully selecting one's environment and social circle is a consistent factor I've observed in many patients who are emotionally fulfilled, supported, and even happy when going through difficult diagnoses or even in the final chapter of their lives. In the pre-pandemic days, we would see this manifest physically with groups of friends who visited our patients' rooms. These patients would often share that they were glad they valued positivity in their friends, as it had brought them significant happiness.

This feeling of shared positivity is a phenomenon that has been studied in the social sciences as well, and is known as *emotional contagion*. An experiment studying this concept monitored a group when there was a member purposefully exhibiting positive or negative energy while the group (the rest of whom were participants) did a task. The group where there was an actor exhibiting positive motions had improved cooperation, decreased conflict, and increased perceived performance. On the other hand, when actors exhibited negative energy, this in turn caused the participants to have negative energy, creating a downward spiral.[121]

Clearly, the emotions exhibited by our friends and others around us have a strong impact on those emotions we exhibit ourselves. A social environment of support, happiness, and positivity will result in one's own life having these qualities, and unfortunately, the opposite is true as well. It can be heartbreaking to see patients going through such difficult diagnoses whose social groups provide pessimism rather than hope. We try to provide that positivity as the patients' doctors, but it can be difficult for our patients in spite of our best efforts.

I felt the effect of emotional contagion every day when I would see Kristy Wharton. She was the patient, but whenever I'd round on her, *she* would make *me* feel better simply through her positive energy.

Unfortunately, the workup revealed that the cause of the biliary tract obstruction was an extremely aggressive form of pancreatic cancer that had spread. We consulted the oncology specialists, who discussed with her the various treatment options and the effect they would have on her, as well as the probability of any improvement or success. After discussing with her oncology team, Mrs. Wharton decided she wanted to value her quality of life rather than go through aggressive treatment options.

Although she was sad, she expressed much gratitude to her medical team as well as her social support system.

The day she was discharged back to her assisted living facility with hospice care, she told her friends when they picked her up from the hospital, "You have all made my life so amazing. I know it must come to an end, but I'd like to spend this final chapter with you all."

We kept in touch after she left the hospital. She would email me pictures of her and her friends going to the beach together or watching a play.

Kristy Wharton passed away seven months after leaving the hospital. I was honored to be invited to her funeral by her family and friends. They all spoke about how even to the very end, she made them laugh.

Chapter 22

Remember, you don't have to be exceptional.

When I met Theresa Garcia, my first thought was how warm her presence was. Even while sick with COVID and having difficulty breathing, she still exuded the sort of kindness typically associated with one's grandmothers; she spoke with a slow, affectionate voice and had crow's feet on the outer corners of her loving brown eyes that came from a lifetime of genuine smiling.

The eighty-six-year-old woman had long, flowing silver hair and wore a simple white robe and sandals. Her face mask was bright white, matching her clothing. Contrasting the simplicity of the outfit were her smartwatch and tablet computer.

Mrs. Garcia had been having fevers for the past three days. She took a COVID test at home and found she was positive, so she began quarantining. Over the next couple days, however, she began to have trouble breathing. She thought she would try taking her inhaler at home and see if her breathing would improve on its own.

However, this morning, her husband noticed that her smile was crooked. At the same time, her smartwatch had beeped, alerting her that her heart rate was faster than normal. Her husband knew these could be signs of a stroke, so he insisted she come to the emergency room.

Thankfully, Mrs. Garcia's symptoms had resolved by the time she came to the emergency room. We obtained an MRI scan of her brain, and our neurology team examined her. We concluded that what she had experienced was a "transient ischemic attack" (TIA) or mini-stroke. This is when the brain temporarily doesn't have enough blood due to a blockage (just like in a stroke), but the blood supply is then restored. TIAs are still quite serious because these patients are at high risk of having a stroke in the future.

As we examined her breathing, we noted that she had wheezes throughout her lung field and her oxygen levels were low. She had a history of asthma, and the COVID infection was likely triggering an asthma exacerbation.

She told me her smartwatch actually monitored her heart rate, and her phone could also produce an EKG strip for me to read. I'm constantly amazed at the innovation smart technology is making in the field of medicine. Whereas diagnosing a heart arrhythmia required close monitoring inpatient or for patients to wear clunky heart monitors, now (some) heart rhythms can be diagnosed with smartwatches.

Theresa unlocked her tablet, and I saw that the background of her phone was a row of houses and buildings behind a river. I asked her if that was her home. She smiled, handed me the tablet, and told me to take a closer look.

I realized that the background was actually a painting! It displayed a row of ordinary houses and buildings on a cloudy morning in what appeared to be a European town a few hundred years ago. In the painting, two women are engaged in everyday chores and several other townsfolk are going about their day.

"This is one of my favorite works of art. I first saw it at a museum during our trip to Amsterdam. It's a painting by Dutch Baroque painter Vermeer called *View of Delft,* which shows typical life in Delft during the Dutch Golden Age. It celebrates the contentedness in the humdrum of everyday life. Vermeer finds beauty in what society considers banal."

Theresa Garcia's passion for art was palpable.

When examining the data from her smartwatch, I saw that Mrs. Garcia had briefly been in an abnormal heart rhythm called atrial fibrillation. I admitted her into the hospital so we could figure out the cause of the TIA, monitor her heart rhythm, and start treatments to help with her breathing and support her oxygen level.

As with every patient, when she was admitted to the hospital, we had asked Mrs. Garcia to clarify her code status.

She had responded with, "If I die, let me leave this life in peace. Please do not do any heroic resuscitative efforts. I have had such an amazing life, Dr. Abbasi. I feel so incredibly lucky to have lived with the bliss and peace I've had."

Mrs. Garcia told me how she was a latecomer to her field of therapy and mental health. She had originally studied to become a librarian. After obtaining her master's in library sciences, she worked in the college library of her local community college.

"Oh, it was a truly wonderful profession! I absolutely cherished helping students find the information they needed to complete their projects, write their essays, and study for their exams," she told me with delight.

In her fifties, she began reading more about the emerging science behind mental health.

"I realized I wanted to become a therapist!" So, she went back to school and obtained a master's degree in psychology and eventually her license to practice as a therapist. "I was a therapist at a psychology clinic for twenty years before I retired. I feel so honored to have been able to guide individuals and families on the path to their happiness."

Despite all of the treatments, the COVID pneumonia began to spread quite aggressively in her lungs. She began feeling breathless and had a bad cough. Over the next forty-eight hours, we continued to increase the amount of oxygen support she was receiving so her lungs could provide her organs with enough oxygen to function. Eventually, she required maximum levels of a high-flow nasal cannula.

I went to her room frequently to check on her over the next day as her breathing became increasingly labored. Mrs. Garcia knew there was a significant prospect of her not surviving the hospitalization, but she still seemed to be at peace and content. Even when faced with her mortality, she did not express any regrets like many other patients had.

Her facial expression was one of pensive serenity. I eventually mustered up the courage to ask her what brought this sense of gratification.

"You seem to be at peace. You have brought upon peace and happiness to so many others during your career. What lessons do you have for others on how they can attain the happiness you have?" I asked her.

"The timeless lesson I have learned, both from my own experience and from caring for others, is that the happiness we seek will *not* come from constantly trying to achieve the next big thing. In our culture, we have created a false narrative that in order to be successful, you have to be above average or exceptional. This is the fundamental issue that drives the unhappiness I have seen in so many who may appear to be outwardly successful," she sagely explained.

Her point resonated well with me. If someone had told me in medical school or residency that I was performing "average" or "mediocre," I would have taken it as a sign of failure. But anyone with a basic understanding of statistics will realize that this sets up most of the population to feel like they're failures if everyone thinks this way. Statistically, not everyone can be above average. Heck, roughly half of all people are below average. But hearing one is below average is interpreted in our minds as a devastating insult.

"My view of the world completely changed when I, as a therapist, began to view the criteria of success as 'happiness' rather than the other metrics our culture perpetrated. We are culturally primed to view captains of industry, famous stars, and superhuman athletes as the successful ones. But in my experience, these aren't the people who are happy."

Theresa Garcia took a couple minutes to catch her breath and take a deep gasp of air through the high-flow machine before continuing.

"I have learned the truly content are the ones who have achieved greatness in areas society deems as mundane. They are dedicated spouses, prioritizing their partners over others. They take pride in raising a happy child. They are giving and devoted friends. They enjoy, but are not overwhelmed, by their jobs. These are the keys to happiness. But you will be hard pressed to find these qualities celebrated on billboards or movie screens."

I nodded in agreement. My own experience with my patients rang true with what she was saying. Some of the patients who have been miserable and full of regret in their death would have been considered successful by traditional metrics. On the other hand, many of my patients who have been at peace in death, looking back with pride on their life, led ordinary lives full of love and fulfillment.

I found that some of the most tragic patients were those who had spent their whole lives chasing what they perceived as "greatness." Typically, these individuals had achieved an above average standing in the domain of their choice. Mr. Kensington and his extreme devotion to his business come to mind. But these patients never seem to find happiness, because every time they get to the next step, they've been conditioned to need to be above average in that new group.

On the other hand, the patients I have seen satisfied at the end of their lives are the ones who may not be the best in their fields, but are content at trying their best and being happy with whatever the results may be. As is evident with other patients you have met in this book, many have indeed achieved greatness, but their successes have been in domains that are not celebrated by society, such as in those of family and friendship. Kristy Wharton and Esther Barnes found happiness in the joy they brought their friends.

These everyday successes are thought of as mundane because anyone could do them if they indeed tried. But not everyone does. In fact, few pursue these goals with the same tenacity with which they pursue other ambitions.

I have seen many miserable patients sacrifice these "simple" achievements in order to pursue those they may or may not achieve and may or may not give them happiness. These patients always regret this bitter misallocation of their lives and express anguish that they weren't better at the more ordinary parts of life.

Perhaps this focus on simple achievements is something some of us learn with age. Researchers have found that focusing on time leads to greater happiness than focusing on money. Additionally, ordinary experiences become increasingly associated with happiness as people get older; ordinary experiences produce as much happiness as extraordinary experiences when people feel they have limited time remaining.[122]

Upon this reflection, I began to realize how truly beautiful the celebration of the everyday was. Suddenly Vermeer's painting *View of Delft* made more sense to me.

French renaissance philosopher Michel de Montaigne once captured this sentiment in his writings, stating that:

> Storming a breach, conducting an embassy, ruling a nation are glittering deeds. Rebuking, laughing, buying, selling, loving, hating and living together gently and justly with your household—and with yourself—not getting slack nor being false to yourself, is something more remarkable, more rare and more difficult. Whatever people may say, such secluded lives sustain in that way duties which are at least as hard and as tense as those of other lives.[123]

Theresa Garcia continued to decline over the next few days. As the infection spread, her organs began to fail. She began to lose her mental awareness but would still have periods of lucidity. During one such period, she told me, "I know that this is the end for me. I am grateful to have lived such a meaningful life. I have helped others find happiness, and this has brought me happiness."

As per her wishes, she was transitioned to hospice care. She passed away peacefully in her sleep a few days later.

Patients like Mrs. Garcia demonstrate wisdom in not striving for some idea of exceptionalism at the expense of one's own joy. The most meaningful moments of our lives come from the most ordinary of scenarios.

Chapter 23

Do not let hatred corrode your soul.

When Jerome Simon first came into the urgent care, he smugly told us that in his eighty-seven years of living, this was the first time he had ever been in the hospital. He didn't take any medications and had never gotten even as much as a physical.

"I'm only coming in because my granddaughter here is forcing me to since the news got all y'all riled up." He gestured at his granddaughter who sat next to him.

"She's a smart lady. You're lucky to have family like her to be there for you," I replied.

"She's all I got now. My brother and I don't get along no more," he said with a soft sigh and looked away.

I caught a glimmer of sadness in his eyes, but it was fleeting and was quickly replaced with the usual playful twinkle.

Mr. Simon's first symptom was mild difficulty breathing. When he first came into the hospital, he required a small level of oxygen support with the nasal cannula. By the third day, his oxygen levels had actually improved significantly. He felt that his breathing was getting easier as well. Both Mr. Simon and myself anticipated that he could be discharged soon.

Unfortunately, the improvement was only temporary. Later that day, his breathing began deteriorating rapidly. His oxygen support needed to be steadily increased over the course of the night. By the next day, we upgraded his oxygen support to a HFNC.

As the severity of his illness increased, his tone changed. His once light demeanor became increasingly sad and regretful. The playful twinkle in his eye was slowly extinguished as the severity of the infection became apparent.

★★★

I visited his room several times during that day to closely monitor how he was doing. He slowly opened up to me, and each time I saw him, he told me more about his life.

"Growing up, my brother and I were inseparable. We did everything together. He was my best friend." Mr. Simon took deep breaths through the HFNC tube between each sentence.

Our eyes met, and I saw that his were red from crying.

"We had a pretty bad falling out in our fifties. We ran the family farm together, you see. We had a big disagreement over certain aspects of the business, and the whole thing spiraled from there."

His Southern drawl was interrupted by the sound of air flowing from the HFNC as he caught his breath after every sentence.

"The argument snowballed, as these things can do, and it switched from being about business to becoming personal. It all seems rather silly now that the whole thing started from an argument about seeds and grains."

With tears in his eyes, he fell into a coughing fit as the HFNC pushed the phlegm that had built up in his nose into his throat. I used a suction to help clear up his airways a bit and make him comfortable.

"I tried calling him last night when my breathing started getting worse. He didn't pick up the phone. I know he hasn't changed his number because it's still his voice on the voicemail." His voice choked as he then said, "I don't think he even knows I've got the COVID yet. I just want to hear his voice again before I have to go.

"I should have never let it come to this!" he exclaimed before another coughing fit.

Mr. Simon passed away later that night.

As per his request, I called his brother on the number Mr. Simon gave me. Unfortunately, I was not able to reach him.

When at death's door, patients share what wracks their conscience, as they are no longer able to suppress it the way they did in life. During the COVID surges, we saw many pass through death's gateway and go through this comprehension of their regrets.

Death thrusts perspective upon us. Some things that appear so urgent in life appear so trifling in death. The most common example of this dichotomy was with patients' experiences of hatred.

Hatred is such a strange feeling to observe as a physician, as it can be so strong and all-encompassing, especially when it is expressed among family members or previously close friends. You see people put so much effort into maintaining the hatred, and you see how much doing so takes out of them, like a fire that requires constant fueling. But you also observe how evanescent it is when, suddenly, that same person is faced with their own mortality. Something that seemed so serious it fueled decades of hatred all of a sudden appears silly or unimportant.

I have seen so many patients, when they are at death's door, be devastated by the regret they have for the hatred they held onto during their lives. Inevitably, they always try to repair the relationship, or at least seek some sort of forgiveness or closure before they die.

It is very rare that they are able to.

Donald Stenson was one of the few patients who was given this rare chance. At fifty-seven, he was one of the younger patients on the internal medicine service hospitalized with COVID-19. He had first come in with just some cough and fever, but he was hospitalized when it was found that the infection had also triggered an exacerbation of his chronic COPD. He was admitted to the wards so we could begin IV steroids as well as nebulized medications.

Over the next couple days, he told me about his best friend growing up, Gerald. Donald and Gerald were inseparable as children. They even went to the same college, and Donald was Gerald's best man at his wedding.

Sadly, they had gotten into a major argument, the details of which Mr. Stenson did not feel inclined to share. After that, they never spoke to each other for ten years.

On the first day of his hospitalization, as he had difficulty gasping for breaths, Donald told me that he regretted letting such an important friendship be ruined by one argument.

"We both said terrible things to each other. I wish I could take it back, but I cannot," he told me.

When I asked if we wanted to call him or reach out in some other way, he declined.

"He should be the one reaching out to me, frankly."

Two nights later, I heard the overhead alarm go off. *Code Blue Alert, room 224*. Donald Stenson's room.

His heart had stopped. We immediately began CPR and resuscitative efforts, including shocks and vasoactive medications.

Donald Stenson was dead for four minutes before we got his heartbeat back.

He was transferred to the ICU where he was closely monitored and eventually removed from the ventilator three days later when his heart and lungs could work without machine support.

I heard that he had been extubated, and I went over to the ICU to check on him. When I approached his room, I saw he was on his phone.

"Gerald, man, it's good to hear your voice. Listen, I'm in the hospital. My heart stopped, and when they were trying to revive me, I had this sudden realization about how stupid our fight was ...."

Tears were streaming down Donald's cheeks. I decided to come by his room later in order to give him some privacy.

The latest medical research tells us that having hatred in one's heart is actually bad for your health. Long-term feelings of hate or prejudice have been associated with the kind of stress that can lead to chronic problems like cancer, hypertension, and Type II diabetes. [124]Furthermore, in studies, individuals with high amounts of hate, such as racists, had low levels of DHEA-S, a hormone that helps repair tissue damage caused by the taxing "fight-or-flight" response they undergo whenever they see the object of their hatred.[125]

And harboring hatred *in one's heart* may not be as metaphorical as you'd think. Researchers in Santa Barbara found that when racists saw individuals of the race that they hate, they had diminished blood pumped through the heart and constriction of the circulatory system.[126]

All this testifies to the very real threat chronic hatred has on our health. Substances that pose similar risks, such as tobacco, contain black box warnings, and as physicians, we actively counsel our patients to quit. We must monitor the feelings in our own hearts, and if we harbor these negative emotions, we must eliminate them before they take over our lives, and eventually end them. If we hold hate in our hearts for any friends or family members, it is in our own health interest to reach out to them and squash the beef. If we cannot do that, then we owe it to ourselves to at least start undergoing therapy so we can instill healthier emotions into our minds.

Failure to do so will corrode both our physical and mental health until we are on our deathbeds and filled with regrets. Broken families and shattered friendships are kept that way in life due to stubbornness, but during the pandemic, we saw so many try—oftentimes in vain—to repair those relationships before they passed. Not all of us will be given a second chance like Donald Stenson was.

Life is too cursory to be spent fueling hatred, only to profoundly regret doing so when it is too late. It is wiser to seek amends when one still has time so they do not lie on their deathbed with such regrets.

Chapter 24

Know you are worthy.

"You are worthy of life, worthy of love," I gently told the frail teenager in the emergency department. His hand felt cold, so I held it with both of mine, trying my best to warm it up. His face was pale, and his eyes were red with swollen lids from crying until he could not form any more tears. He came in after having ingested a bottle of acetaminophen. As soon as he had swallowed the pills, he regretted it and came to the hospital. We immediately gave him activated charcoal in order to prevent absorption of the acetaminophen and n-acetyl cysteine to prevent toxicity from the ingestion. Luckily, he had come to the hospital in time, and we were able to prevent any damage.

After stabilizing him physically, our next step was to stabilize his mental health crisis. We would admit him to the hospital so he could work with the psychology team. As the internal medicine doctor, the best thing I could do for him was to make sure he was in the best mindset to benefit as much as possible from the psychological care he would receive. I thought back to a patient I had met in my first week as a doctor, who taught me how to do this effectively.

Lisa Aaron had gone fifty-four years without having any major medical problems. She would come into the hospital for her yearly checkup, without even so much as a single abnormal lab finding.

It therefore took her by surprise when she began having a really bad headache one evening. She had experienced the occasional headache in the past and had resolved them with Tylenol. Thinking it was a migraine or tension headache, she took a Tylenol and tried to sleep it off. But she could not sleep.

The pain increased. It began in just her forehead, but it was now spreading to her entire head. The pain bore down into her skull. Her neck was stiff like someone had put a collar on her.

"It was literally the worst headache of my life!" she told me.

By midnight the pain was unbearable. She called 911 and was brought in to the emergency department. As soon as she arrived, we obtained a CT scan of her brain. It showed bleeding in the area between the brain and the tissue covering the brain. This is called a subarachnoid hemorrhage and is often caused by an aneurysm, or bulging blood vessel, bursting open.

Lisa was admitted to the intensive care unit for constant cardiac and neurologic monitoring. We started continuous IV medications to control her blood pressure. The neurosurgeon on call took her to the OR to repair the aneurysm through a process called endovascular coiling.

I saw her the next morning in her room recovering after the surgery. The top of her head was bandaged. She smiled up at me when I sat down on the stool next to her bed.

"It's good to see you, Dr. Abbasi! The neurosurgeon yesterday explained to me how serious the bleed was, but it looks like I made it through."

"How are you feeling?" I asked her.

"The pain is all gone. I was scared at first when I saw how big the bleed in my brain was. Before the brain surgery, I had this weird moment of clarity. I abruptly had this realization of how gratifying my life is. I have a lot more that I'd like to do in life, but I'm grateful for what I've been able to do thus far," she told me as she grasped the railings on the bed to sit up.

"Would you feel comfortable sharing with me what has brought your life fulfillment?" I asked her.

"I work as a crisis response counselor who cares for suicidal individuals. It is a very tough job. At times it can be quite emotionally draining. But it is also extremely rewarding. I'm at the point where people I have helped end up reaching out to me years later. Now they have families and whole lives. That brings me so much joy."

Lisa's eyes welled up, and she used a napkin to wipe them.

"All I do is make sure people know that they are worthy. Most of the individuals undergoing this crisis have lost sight of, or have a completely warped view of their self-worth. I remind them that they are worthy. Worthy of life, worthy of love.

"This is a lesson I learned long ago," she continued. "You must consider yourself unconditionally worthy."

She looked up at me and held my hand.

"I'd like to share with you how I learned this if you'd like to hear."

I could feel the warmth from the grasp even through the latex medical gloves. I nodded.

"Yes, I'd really like to hear."

"When I was in college, I was in a dark place. My mother had just died. I felt ostracized by those around me because of my race. I went up to the top floor of the university tower with the intention of jumping off. Every flight of stairs, I'd think to myself, *If only I didn't have the skin color I did. The hair I did. If only I could fit in and belong.*

"As I made it to the rooftop, I walked out. There was a custodian there. He was also Black. He took one look at my face and must have figured out what I intended on doing. Or at least he knew I needed help. He grabbed my shoulders, looked me straight in the eyes, and said, 'My child, you are worthy of life. Do not let others ever take away the knowledge that you are worthy from your heart.'

"Now I have made it my life's mission to uplift others with the knowledge that they too are worthy. Just the way they are. Worthy of life and love."

The psychological trait that Lisa was able to astutely identify that was lacking in the individuals she was helping was *self-worth* or *self-acceptance*. Importantly, this is different from self-esteem. Self-esteem describes how you think and feel about yourself. Self-worth is a more global quality that encompasses knowing and believing in your worth as a person.[127] Self-worth is an element of the self-compassion that Samia Khan taught us about. This is an absolutely important quality to have, as I have seen it emanate from my patients who lead lives of meaning and purpose.

It seems so incredibly basic at first glance. *Of course, I know I am worthy as a human being.* But compare how you treat your own worth to the worth of others in order to truly determine whether you've effectively instilled this into your life. You may find that you are far kinder to others than you are to yourself. We overlook the shortcomings of others, and we may be exceptionally hard on ourselves.

A mindset of knowing one's own self-worth is also protective for one's mental health. A study evaluating self-acceptance in college students found that those with higher levels of self-acceptance were less prone to depression.[128] It's a rather intuitive link, but it has important ramifications. Of course, the etiologies of mental health disease are multifactorial, and mindfulness practices are not a substitute for medical therapy for those that need it. Regardless, there is clear value in strengthening our sense of self-worth.

As physicians, we often have to care for patients as they go through mental health crises, oftentimes after suicide attempts. When I care for a suicidal patient, I make sure to reaffirm their sense of self-worth using elements of positive language and cognitive therapy in order to get them to the point where they accept themselves as worthy of care to heal their psychological wounds. I have learned from Lisa Aaron, always reminding my patients that they are worthy of life, worthy of love.

This is something we can teach ourselves. It can be developed through many of the habits we've learned from other patients we've met. For instance, self-worth appears to actually be a trait we are able to cultivate using mindfulness techniques. Psychologists have found positive correlations between mindfulness, self-esteem, and unconditional self-acceptance. Significantly, they note that mindfulness skills may offer a means to cultivate unconditional self-acceptance.[129]

"I am not sure what causes us to forget we are worthy. Maybe it is something conditioned by society. I know some of my clients have told me they felt that love from their parents, spouses, or loved ones was related to whether they met certain expectations," Lisa pondered.

The ongoing research on this topic may support Lisa's hypothesis. Psychologists studying self-worth note that conditional parental regard based on certain expectations leads us to believe that love from parents is unstable and unreliable, which may then form the foundation for a view of the self as unworthy of love.[130] We may cognitively know that our parents love us no matter what, but the language they use when we are still kids equipped with rapidly developing brains shapes how our minds are hardwired to feel worthy of love. Scientific research on effective parenting is still in its infancy, but I suspect that as we learn more about our psychology, we'll be able to offer more practical guidance to parents. In the meantime, just as we learn to accept ourselves, faults and all, we also learn to accept our parents in all their imperfections, as, just like us, they are trying their best to do right in this journey of life.

Dr. Brené Brown, speaker and researcher on social work, eloquently notes in her book *Braving the Wilderness*, "True belonging and self-worth are not goods; we don't negotiate their value with the world. The truth about who we are lives in our hearts. Our call to courage is to protect our wild heart against constant evaluation, especially our own. No one belongs here more than you."[131]

I repeated Lisa Aaron's essential phrase to the pale, slim teenager sitting in front of me in the emergency department. "No matter what happens in life, remember that you are worthy of life, worthy of love."

His cold hand began to thaw with warmth, and color once again saturated his face.

He said, "Thank you, doc. I think I'm ready to get better."

Chapter 25

Know transcendence.

Sara Hakim was 108 years old when I met her in the emergency department. I was shocked when I read her age in her chart. The years may have inscribed wrinkles on her face, but they were overshadowed by a distinctive brilliance of a youthful mind. She wore a long brown *abaya* robe; her hair was loosely wrapped in a white headscarf; and in her right hand, she held a set of Islamic prayer beads called *tasbih*. Creases of experience crossed her forehead, but in between, her skin glowed a fair olive. She looked like she was in her seventies, but her energy level was that of someone in their thirties.

She spoke a little bit of English, yet she preferred to speak Arabic, as that was her native tongue. In our hospital, we have tablet computers in the patient room where you can select the language the patient speaks and a live translator will be brought online via video chat to assist with communication.

Through the translator, Mrs. Hakim told me she had first noticed feeling chills and a sore throat the day before. After she began to struggle with breathing, she decided to come into the hospital. She was diagnosed with COVID with a concurrent bacterial pneumonia.

We admitted her to the hospital since she needed oxygen support as well as IV antibiotics for the pneumonia. As I started to broach the subject of code status, she immediately stated that she wanted to be DNR.

"If I am to die, then let me die as is written. I have a relationship with death and will not resist when it comes," she said in Arabic.

After organizing all the logistics for her hospital admission, I went to the waiting room to update Mrs. Hakim's daughter. After I went through the plan with her, she thanked me profusely and gave me a delicious piece of baklava.

When I went to Mrs. Hakim's room the next morning during rounds, I saw she was sitting on the bed cross-legged. The window was open and the orange glow of the sunrise shone into the room, casting a glimmer across her face. Her daughter was in the room, sitting on the chair opposite of the bed.

Mrs. Hakim's eyes were closed, and she was softly saying a meditative chant in Arabic, occasionally stopping to take a breath through the nasal cannula supporting her breathing. The tasbih was in her hand, and with every chant she would slide a bead over. The hymn she chanted in a soft voice almost seemed to harmonize with the hum of the nasal cannula device.

I waited in the hallway for a couple of minutes so I wouldn't disturb her. When I walked in, she gave me a smile. We discussed the plan for the day and the treatments she would be receiving from the respiratory therapy team.

Afterwards, I asked her if she would feel comfortable telling me about the meditation she had been doing when I entered the room.

"That is *dhikr*," she said. "It is a form of Sufi mindfulness where I chant and meditate on the greater power and remind myself of my purpose."

"My mother does this every day, doc," her daughter said. "These practices are what has kept her mind sharper than all of ours all these years!"

Sara Hakim nodded. "It has been an important act to root my life in essence."

I asked her if she would tell me more about this philosophy.

"Doing Sufi practices, such as *muraqabah* (meditation) and *dhikr* (chanting) help me reach a state of transcendence. This is when your mind rises above the intricacies of the now, and you are one with your soul. Achieving this state of transcendence is paramount, as it reminds you to think beyond yourself. It clears your mind, unburdens it from what is limiting your thinking, and allows you to truly think freely.

"This is not something just for the religious. And you don't have to be a Sufi sheikh to experience it! Anyone who has experienced a state of clarity and flow when meditating or doing what they love knows this state."

Mrs. Hakim was not the first patient to tell me about reaching this transcendent state. Ju Lao would speak about reaching a similar level of consciousness when meditating, where her mind would "reach a state of flow, just like a river."

Interestingly, other patients had mentioned this state to me in contexts outside of religion or purposeful mindfulness. For instance, Bart Scully spoke about reaching a transcendent state as he would write, when he felt so "in the zone" that he would completely lose track of time. John McDonald described feeling "fully immersed" when he was painting. I have met musicians who have described this state when playing their instrument and athletes who describe this state when playing their sport.

I've found that when I'm thinking through a complex medical diagnosis for a patient, I feel this state of flow as I work through the problem in my head.

Psychologists have dubbed this phenomenon as "flow state." It was first studied by psychologist Mihaly Robert Csikszentmihalyi who was intrigued by artists who would get lost in their craft when making art. He noted that they entered a state of focus that amounts to absolute absorption in what one is doing, and a heightened overall experience.[132] Since then, flow state has become widely recognized as a universal state of transcendence that a master achieves when thoroughly invested in their craft at a particular moment.

Neuroscientists studying brains that are in flow state have also found an increase in certain neurotransmitters, which are the chemicals in the brain that mediate certain processes. Specifically, this state increases norepinephrine, dopamine, serotonin, anandamide, and endorphins.

There are also happiness-causing and performance-enhancing chemicals that increase creativity. Norepinephrine increases our focus, allowing us to ignore background distraction. Serotonin and dopamine allow us to realize a sense of satisfaction and meaning in what we are doing. And anandamide has been associated with creative and lateral thinking.[133]

Although this is an area of ongoing research, psychological researchers have found that achieving the flow state when working through complex problems is associated with increased performance for mathematics students,[134] programmers,[135] and musicians.[136]

Achieving the flow state also results in increased performance in elite athletes. Significantly, studies have found that this is something that can be trained to achieve tangible changes. Psychological interventions to improve flow states and performance consistently resulted in either quantitative or qualitative increases in performance.[137] This has significant implications for us, as it means we can work on practices to achieve this state.

Psychologist Csikszentmihalyi notes, "Although the flow experience appears to be effortless, it is far from being so. It often requires strenuous physical exertion, or highly disciplined mental activity. It does not happen without the application of skilled performance ... the optimal experience is thus something we make happen."[138]

A study on actors and flow state during theater performances found that they could achieve flow state through immense concentration exercises and focus.[139] The obvious connection that experts have made is that engaging in meditation and other mindfulness practices allows one to achieve this level of concentration. Though studies are ongoing, it appears that meditative states and flow states are quite related and possibly the same state just in different circumstances.

Mrs. Hakim's daughter told me that when her mother used to live in Iraq, she was a Sufi mystic teacher. She would teach her pupils mindfulness techniques that they could apply to their lives in order to achieve mastery in their respective trades.

I asked Mrs. Hakim if she could tell me what she would tell her students in achieving this transcendent state.

"It will be a different path for everyone, but first you must develop a relationship with your mind. Do this through some mindfulness activity, such as meditation or *dhikr*. Do this every day by integrating it into your daily schedule. Then your mind will become trained to have focus.

"Once you have done this, find what you are passionate about. Approach this craft with the goal of mastering it. As you train or work, focus your mind. You can even engage in the mindfulness activity as you work."

Ju Lao showed me that in order to enter the meditative state of flow, one must have a great degree of focus.

"Close your eyes and breathe deeply in and out. Know your body by feeling the ground underneath you and each breath come in and out. Know your mind by recognizing the thoughts in it. Then considerately clear your mind of all thoughts that are extraneous. As other thoughts pop up, acknowledge them, but gently remove them. Focus on a singular setting that brings you tranquility. For me, it is the riverbank where I used to play as a child. Others may use a mantra."

The transcendent state of flow Sara Hakim told me about relied on a similar practice of making a singular thing the locus of your attention. The effectiveness of this technique has been confirmed by wellness experts researching these states. In an interesting experiment, researchers in Iran found that having athletes engage in meditation as part of their practice improved their ability to achieve flow state during a match.[140] Neuroscientists looking at brain waves through an electroencephalography machine found that mantra-based meditation practices elicited the same brain waves as those observed in flow state.[141]

Scientists studying this state have observed individuals engaging in meditative practices. They found that the physical state of the body actually changes, with slowed breathing, respiratory suspension, and reduced muscle activity. In one study where scientists monitored the brain's electrical activity in flow state, they found increased alpha power during transcendence, which refers to the brain waves classically associated with restfulness and tranquility.[142]

Achieving a transcendental state of flow appears to be critical to leading a meaningful life, as it allows us to be fully involved in the present. It also gives us a sense of fulfillment in what we are doing. Researchers have found that individuals who achieve the flow state had a higher level of job satisfaction and sense of contentment in their career.[143]

Flow state could also have implications for physical health. One study found that among African Americans who are at higher risk for cardiovascular disease, engaging in meditation resulted in reduced carotid atherosclerosis, or hardening of their carotid arteries.[144] Researchers have also found that meditation reduces stress, resulting in lower levels of cortisol, the stress hormone. This, in turn, resulted in lower levels of cardiovascular disease.[145]

It would not be far-fetched to say that Sara Hakim's transcendental mindfulness played a big role in her long life and relatively good health, even when she was over a hundred years old. The field of medicine has been catching up to this research as well. Physicians now regularly recommend integration of mindfulness activities in order to decrease stress and cultivate a myriad of health benefits.

Sara Hakim regrettably continued to worsen despite all of the therapies. It was easy to forget she was 108 years old given how sharp she was, but the mortality of COVID in her age group in the pre-vaccine era was sadly quite dismal.

Eventually, it was clear that she would not recover from this illness and her body would continue to shut down. We complied with her wishes, and together with her family, transitioned her to comfort care measures in the hospital.

Toward the end, Sara Hakim was not always able to be mentally present. She was incredibly weak as her organs began failing, and she was not able to maintain her oxygen level on maximum support with the high-flow nasal cannula. Even in such a delirious state, she would often recite the words for her *dhikr* as she lay in bed.

As she prepared to leave this world, we did our best to make sure she was comfortable and not in pain. The next evening, I was in the room to examine her and make sure she was at peace. The window was open, and the orange glow of the sunset illuminated her bed.

As I listened to her heart with my stethoscope, she suddenly opened her eyes. She clasped her hands together in front of her chest and said her words of mindfulness. Then, she took a deep breath in, shuddered, and passed away.

"Time of death: 7:14 p.m.," I stated.

Her nurse gently covered her with a blanket.

Chapter 26

Recognize we are all one consciousness.

"Let go of your mind and then be mindful."—Rumi[146]

Bandile Mokoena was, in many ways, the average patient who comes into urgent care, if there could ever be such a thing. He was in his fifties, did not have any significant medical history besides hypertension and high cholesterol, and had only previously come into the hospital to see his primary care.

He first felt pain in his abdomen when he ate his lunch. Over the next two days, the pain began to worsen. The crampy feeling whenever he'd try to eat made him lose his appetite, and he decided to come into the hospital to see what was going on. Upon my physical examination, I saw that his abdomen was tender in the right upper quadrant. I did an exam maneuver called Murphy's Sign that allows you to examine the patient's gallbladder by having them take a deep breath in while you press on the right side of their abdomen underneath their ribs.

"Ouch!" he yelped when I pressed down.

A positive Murphy's Sign meant that his gallbladder was likely inflamed.

We did an ultrasound of his abdomen in order to evaluate the cause of the pain and check his gallbladder. His exam and labs suggested that there may have been gallstones obstructing the biliary tract draining his gallbladder.

The ultrasound showed that there was indeed a gallstone blocking the common bile duct. However, as some of the other labs began to result, to his surprise, he was found to be COVID positive.

"Now that I think about it, I have been feeling quite tired and cold for the past few days. Maybe that was the COVID," he noted.

Regardless, reassuringly he was not having any trouble breathing.

We made a plan to relieve the obstruction caused by the stone in the common bile duct via a procedure called an Endoscopic retrograde cholangiopancreatography (ERCP), which can be used to extract the obstructing stone. After this procedure, our general surgery colleagues would remove the gallbladder with a procedure called a cholecystectomy so that this kind of obstruction would not recur in the future.

After discussing the plan and meeting with the specialist gastroenterologist who would be doing the ERCP, Bandile agreed to proceed with the procedure.

The morning of the procedure, I rounded on Bandile's room to check on him and see if he had any last-minute questions.

"I'm ready, doc. Let's get this done so I can eat!" he said.

Over the next day, both the procedure and surgery went well. The plan was to monitor Mr. Mokoena's post-op progress and slowly advance his diet over the next day.

"Our hope is that you'll be able to go home soon over the next couple days!" I told him to his delight.

That night, I was awakened by the alarm in the overnight call room. "Code Blue, room 8776" blared on the loudspeaker. I grabbed my stethoscope and ran to Bandile's room.

As soon as I entered, I saw that Bandile had no pulse. He was not breathing and had no heartbeat. We immediately began CPR.

The heart monitor pads showed that his heart had gone into a fatal rhythm called ventricular tachycardia.

"Push one milligram epinephrine and charge to 200J," I told the team.

The sound of an electrical hum filled the room as the pads charged.

"Clear!" I called before shocking Bandile's heart.

His body contracted, and his back briefly arched up as the shock was administered. I looked back at the heart monitor. He was still in ventricular tachycardia.

We resumed chest compressions. "Let's get STAT CBC, CMP, and ABG with all electrolytes," I requested of the phlebotomist who entered the room.

"Push 300 mg amiodarone and charge to 200J" I said, preparing to shock him again. The hum of the charging pads filled the room again.

"Clear!" *Shock.*

We resumed chest compressions. A few seconds later, a groan filled the room. I looked at the bed. It was Bandile slowly opening his eyes and moving his arms! I looked at the heart monitor, and his heart had reverted back to a normal rhythm.

The tension in the room evaporated, and we all felt a sense of relief.

Bandile Mokoena had been dead for three minutes.

He was moved to the intensive care unit where he was found to have a collapsed lung, called a pneumothorax, that had likely irritated the heart and caused the fatal arrhythmia. A chest tube was placed to help the lung re-expand, and he recovered well. A day later, he was miraculously back to his baseline self.

I went to Bandile's room in the ICU to see how he was doing.

"Doctor Abbasi, thank you for all that you and everyone did. You all did such an amazing job, and everyone worked together like clockwork. It was very impressive," he said to me with a knowing smile on his face, waiting for me to ask the obvious question.

Fine, I'll bite, I thought. "How do you know that, Mr. Mokoene? You were out the whole time!"

"When I died, I was looking down and saw that you were all working hard to bring me back. I saw you shock my heart, and I saw the nurses doing chest compressions," he told me.

Tears rolled down his cheeks.

I asked him if he would feel comfortable sharing his experience with me.

"I was lifted up and could see the entire room. I saw everyone doing CPR and administering medicines and shocks. Then I was called up to go even higher. I went through a tunnel. As I was pulled through the tunnel, my entire life went through my mind, almost like a highlight reel. I saw myself first learning to walk. My first day of school. I saw the day I was married. My son being born."

I handed Bandile a tissue as his tears flowed out of his eyes. He was crying, but he had a slight smile on his face as he described the next part.

"Then I became part of the greater light. I do not know how to describe it to you. Words cannot encompass the feelings and emotions this light conveyed. All of humankind's consciousness was one. I could feel the collective knowledge, collective pain, collective joy, and collective love. This does not adequately describe what it was like. It felt like I was back to where I had come from before. The common origin of all people."

Throughout the COVID pandemic, I have had seven patients who have technically died (no heartbeat) and were brought back. Of those, three of them have been able to share their experience with me. (Four of them did not remember anything and felt like they had just gone to sleep and woken up.)

These three patients shared a remarkably similar experience. They all described looking down and seeing the critical care team doing CPR. They all described re-experiencing key moments in their lives. They all described going through a tunnel or toward some light. And, most significantly, they all noted becoming part of a greater consciousness and discovering the unity in all mankind.

What happens in these moments is a fairly controversial topic in the field of neuroscience and medicine. Near-death experiences are reported by up to 40 percent of individuals who come close to death.[147] However, it has been suggested by many scientists and physicians that the phenomenon of near-death experiences is one simply caused by low oxygen levels in the brain, hormone levels during stress, and neurotransmitter release in the brain.[148]

Supporting this is that near-death experiences among patients are not universal, although they may have similar qualities. Researchers suggest that some aspects of near-death experiences, such as going through a tunnel, are culture specific.[149]

On the other hand, scientists investigated cases of individuals who claimed to have a near-death experience and found that patients who *really were* close to death were more likely than those who were not to report an enhanced perception of light and enhanced cognitive powers.[150]

Neuroscientists point out that brain function largely ceases during cardiac arrest, so it is strange that such lucid thought processes and memory formation can occur without brain function.[151]

I do not know if the experiences my patients have shared with me are products of a greater mental state, or just chemicals in the brain, or both. I do know that in my patients who have experienced such phenomena, all three have instilled positive changes in their lives, including volunteering at a charity or spending more time with their family. Longitudinal studies following patients years after having near-death experiences after cardiac arrest note positive transformational processes with changing life-insight and the disappearance of fear of death, equivalent to roughly twenty years of psychotherapy.[152]

And I do believe there is some value in knowing that all of these patients describe experiencing some greater light and consciousness that teaches them all human beings are one people. These individuals have experienced a major perspective shift, akin to an astronaut going to space and looking back at the Earth to realize our insignificant place in the universe.

Interestingly, I have observed a similar phenomenon in one more patient. Jillian Swan was in the emergency department when I met her. She lay in the gurney in awe. "It began with an increased perception of the world, with all the sounds around me taking on a beautiful, visual form, almost like looking through a prism. As the hour passed, I saw that I was part of a far greater consciousness. This human experience is a shared one, and we are all connected through this singular consciousness.

My own conscience was expanded, and I saw many different perspectives that make up this woven connectedness we call life."

Thirty-two-year-old Jillian, unlike Bandile, was not going through a near-death experience. Rather, she was tripping on LSD. Her friends had brought her to the Emergency Department when she began feeling palpitations. Reassuringly, a workup revealed that her heart was healthy, and we gave her a safe place to recover from her trip.

I met another patient who unfortunately developed pancreatitis while on psilocybin (known commonly as magic mushrooms). She recovered well in the hospital and is now doing well.

She shared with me that when on psilocybin, "I attained a greater state of understanding. There is a cosmos all around us and life in all things. We are all a shared humanity, and the universe has a plan for us all."

I'm glad her pancreatitis didn't ruin her trip ....

Those of you who have personally or have friends who have engaged in psychedelics may endorse a similar experience. My limited exposure to "psychonauts" (the nickname that some in the psychedelic community have given themselves) is primarily when they come in to the hospital while suffering a very bad trip. When speaking to these patients, they often tell me that a major appeal of psychedelics is achieving this cosmic realization of our shared consciousness.

I have not personally ever engaged in any psychedelics and would not ever recommend them to any of my patients. Firstly, psychedelics, such as LSD and psilocybin, are illegal in the country I live in (the United States). Additionally, more research is required to assess the safety profiles of these substances in a regulated manner. Unfortunately, research on this matter has been stalled for decades, as the historical association with the anti-Vietnam war movement led to all psychedelics being banned in the US. Over the past half century, research funding and the study of psychedelics as clinical agents has been virtually stopped.[153] This ban remains as of publication time.

Nonetheless, the last decade has seen a second wave of research into psychedelics. As study reemerges on psychedelic substances, there is some fascinating research that describes how psychedelics may have some role in the treatment of psychiatric disorders or in palliative care sometime in the future.[154]

Scientists exploring where in the brain psychedelics work have found that they act in a network of the brain called the "default mode network," which is a neural network of higher-functioning executive areas in the brain. Amazingly, this is actually the same network of brain areas that mediated the state of transcendence Sara Hakim taught us about.

The major nexus that mediates state is the medial prefrontal cortex.[155] You may recall that this is the same area of the brain that lights up during the gratitude practice Ms. Boiko taught us about, which functions to set the context of our lives. Psychologists exploring the possibility of psilocybin use in severe forms of depression have found that it results in decreased amygdala activation, again just like the studies in gratitude practices we discussed earlier.[156]

Another promising application is in that of palliative care of dying patients, such as those with a terminal diagnosis of cancer. There is some preliminary evidence that psilocybin-assisted therapy may produce an antidepressant and anxiolytic response, and improvements in cancer-related anxiety, depression, and suicidal ideation. Due to an awareness of this common consciousness that we've discussed above, there is even some thought that psilocybin can help with existential distress and spiritual well-being.[157]

Regardless of whether this transcendent experience is due to a mystical enlightenment at death or chemicals flooding the brain, perhaps it is not necessary to have a brush with death or ingest mind-altering substances in order to realize our common humanity. I suspect that if we live our lives with the mindset of our shared consciousness, we will open ourselves up to those around us and do more for each other rather than live for only ourselves.

Chapter 27

Deliberately live a life of meaning.

When I entered Jane Erica's room in the urgent care, it was full of life, with the energy of a park rather than a hospital room. Two little girls chased each other around the room, their laughter echoing in the hallway of the hospital. Five middle-aged men and women of different ethnic backgrounds sat in chairs around the bed, holding Mrs. Erica's hands. In the center of all the commotion was ninety-two-year-old Jane Erica on the patient bed. Her gray hair flowed to her waist, interweaving with a bright red scarf. She wore a maroon gown and gold bracelets on either wrist. My first thought was that the whole scene looked rather like a painting from the Italian renaissance.

Mrs. Erica had started feeling breathless a couple days ago. She had thought nothing of it, as most of her family had received the first dose of the COVID vaccine, which had just been released the previous month. She was scheduled to receive her first shot in a few weeks, but what she did not account for was that her grandchildren had not been vaccinated and had served as vectors for the infection.

She decided to come to the urgent care when her breathing continued to worsen over the next couple days. She messaged her cardiologist through the patient portal, who recommended she come into the hospital. She had been seeing her cardiologist for years for a heart disease called *heart failure with reduced ejection fraction* where the heart can't pump blood forward as robustly as it needs to. Because of her medical history, her cardiologist was concerned both because she may be having a heart failure exacerbation as well as because she was at high risk for severe COVID infection due to her medical history.

As I examined her, I found she was, indeed, suffering from a heart failure exacerbation. I began to tell her that she would need to be admitted to the hospital so we could treat the COVID as well as reduce the fluid building up behind her heart, but as soon as I got halfway through my sentence, the whole room erupted in questions. I looked around at what felt like a sea of worried faces.

Luckily for me, Mrs. Erica spoke up. She had a soft, gentle voice, but it seemed to fill up the whole room, cutting across the commotion.

"Now, now. Settle down, everyone. Let's just all listen to what the young doctor has to say. I hear they're making 'em smart these days," she said while winking at me.

In the coming days, Mrs. Erica would love telling me all about her family. She could not have children of her own, so she and her husband had begun fostering children after they got married.

"We could not have predicted the sense of meaning our children would give our lives. I mean, sure Tim [her husband] and I had wanted children, and we were always told by other parents how it changed their lives. But we did not realize the extent of it until we began fostering children. Really, our children have completely elevated our life," Jane shared.

The experience had had such a profound significance on the couple that they decided to adopt the children they were caring for and fully raise them as their own. Mrs. Erica would go on to work at her local adoption agency so that she could help orphans find homes.

When I confirmed her code status, Jane Erica simply told me, "I know because of my heart and other chronic medical conditions, the chances of bringing me back are slim. And even if they're able to, I'd have no life. I'd like to die with some dignity.

"I feel so lucky to have lived such a great life. My children have given my life meaning, and I found great purpose in helping mothers find children over my career."

The infection progressed rapidly in Mrs. Erica. By the end of the week, she was on the maximum oxygen support we could provide, and was still unable to maintain the oxygen levels needed. Additionally, her kidneys had failed, and we had to begin dialysis in order to control the amount of fluid in her body to prevent a severe heart failure exacerbation.

As her body failed, so did her mind. Although she would have periods of lucidity, these became increasingly infrequent. She was started on comfort care measures.

Once when I was in the room, she suddenly woke up. She had tears in her eyes. I asked her what was wrong.

"I am just so happy, doctor. I've lived such a wonderful life filled with love and meaning," she told me, tears in her eyes and a big smile on her lips.

Jane Erica passed away comfortably in her sleep that night.

She clearly lived a life where she found meaning in finding homes for children without them. Having or caring for children may be a rather prototypical manner of finding meaning in one's life, but it is obviously not the only way.

Among the patients whose stories I have shared with you over the last twenty-six chapters, the common theme among those who met death with a sense of fulfillment was that they lived a life of meaning, whatever that may have meant for them. This is a constant motif I have observed in every patient death I have encountered as a physician—where the patient was *ready* for death.

Captain Greg found meaning in serving his country. Knowing death and the fragility of life instilled in him an appreciation for focusing on what matters.

Bart Scully found meaning in his writing and in the journey of always attempting every day to create amazing works through regular, incremental progress.

Vira Boiko found meaning through gratitude. When life was at its darkest, having a gratitude-oriented mindset allowed her to once again fill her life with both contentment and purpose.

Maria and José Sanchez found meaning in their marriage. The immense friendship they shared brought them such bliss and made them inseparable in life and death.

Andre Abara found meaning in standing up for what was right. Having a solid set of principles to live his life by ensured he never regretted the way he treated others.

Dr. Hatake found meaning in treating patients with positivity. Unshakeable optimism allowed him to overcome every obstacle life threw at him.

Luke Williams found meaning in serving his community. He maximized the experience of life by taking something of value from every encounter and individual.

Nicole Lin found meaning by following her dream to be a journalist. She learned that a life of meaning is one where you follow your own dream rather than one imposed upon you by others or society.

Ju Lao found meaning by studying the intersection of Buddhism and technology. Her philosophy of *being as water is* gave her the flexibility and strength to navigate life with a sense of mindfulness.

Justin Jones and Mrs. Hargreeves found meaning in civil rights advocacy. They fought to break the cycle of hatred, as they knew a life of meaning is one of coexistence and love.

Esther Barnes found meaning in her friendships. She knew that a fulfilled life is one of elevating those around you.

Samia Khan found meaning through living a life of self-compassion, knowing that a life of contentment is one where you are kind to yourself.

Dr. Francisco found meaning in simplicity, realizing that in life, one must not be weighed down by excess baggage.

Laila Ali found meaning in helping survivors of abuse, guiding others through the darkest time in their lives to the light at the end of the tunnel.

Professor Costner found meaning in contributing to his scientific field.

Kristy Wharton found meaning in bringing laughter to her friends.

Lisa Aaron found meaning through self-worth, ensuring that the individuals she helped knew they were worthy.

Sara Hakim found meaning through achieving transcendence. She knew that a life of meaning is one of mindful immersion in one's passions.

Researchers have found that on the subject of mortality, human beings fear an incomplete and meaningless life more than death itself. They may use psychological defense mechanisms when they are living, but these do not lend themselves readily as protective barriers against the existential fear of death. The one alleviating factor for the existential dread of death appears to be focusing on living a significant and fulfilling life.[158]

Psychologists have coined the term "self-actualization" to refer to the sense of fulfillment and finding meaning in life.[159] Psychologist Abraham Maslow is famous for creating a "hierarchy of needs" that individuals work on fulfilling. At the bottom are basic needs of humans that must be met (e.g. food, shelter, security). Once one achieves those, they work on "the belongingness and love needs." Once one has achieved a degree of belongingness, the next level is "the esteem needs," where the person will seek a sense of competence and recognition. Only when the basics are met is the person at the most advanced summit of the hierarchy of needs and primed to achieve self-actualization.[160]

Self-actualization appears to be the common thread amongst patients who are at peace with their death. Through self-actualization, one focuses on something larger than oneself and reaches the state of self-transcendence. According to Maslow, self-transcendence occurs at the "very highest and most inclusive or holistic levels of human consciousness."[161]

As I observe my patients at death, I find that this "something larger" may be love, ideology, community, or a social cause. These patients have a transcendental perspective on their life. They've risen above self-centered thinking and have lived their life for something larger than them.

Upon reflection at the numerous patients I've seen pass away, I posit that finding this level of meaning in life is an absolute requirement for dying with a sense of fulfillment and gratification.

But it's important to note that this likely reflects underlying mindset rather than achievement itself. Many of the patients we've met, such as best-selling authors, social justice activists, and nonprofit leaders, have achieved remarkable things that have impacted so many around them.

However, most of the patients described in this book, and that I've met on the wards, have found meaning in what others may view as mundane. For example, many fulfilled patients have found meaning in love, be it for one's spouse (such as the Sanchezes), one's children (such as Mrs. Erica), or one's friends (such as Mrs. Barnes). Love is something that is accessible to most of us blessed with family, friends, or significant others, but fulfillment takes the wisdom of prioritizing that love. Otherwise, I've seen many patients lonely and desolate in death, pleading for a chance to experience love as they die (such as Mr. Kensington).

As Theresa Garcia showed us, the wise among us know that chasing a concept of exceptionality at the expense of what is truly important in life does not lead to a full life.

Life is short and full of surprises. Try to predict as much as you can, but you'll never know, for instance, when the next pandemic is coming. Our existence is too abbreviated to live an empty life.

Before she died, Jane Erica shared with me, "I tell all my children, think about the kind of life you'd be proud of looking back on when you're dying. What would provide you with meaning so you can be fulfilled when it is your time to go? Now go out and live that life."

Epilogue

You will die. But first you will live.

Steep cliffs overlook the Pacific Ocean toward the north of La Jolla, California. Strong gusts of wind carry gliders with colorful sails toward the shining line in the horizon where golden sky meets the blue sea. The air is filled with the laughter of kids and the spice of barbecue as families prepare picnics in the lawn next to the gliderport overlooking the beach. Lovers sit on the edge of the cliff, holding hands as they take in the majestic view.

The Torrey Pines Gliderport has become one of my favorite places over the course of the pandemic. It happens to be on my way home from work, and I often find myself stopping there with my colleagues to relax and meditate after a particularly tough shift. The turmoil and tension of the hospital wards during COVID surges was in stark juxtaposition with tranquility and joy of the park. Watching the sun set over the ocean from the cliffs allowed us to decompress from difficult days.

As COVID cases decreased and the hospital began to have some semblance of normalcy, the administration restarted the weekly Grand Rounds conference. It's over video conference now, which means the fervent debate is replaced with reminding other physicians that their mics are off when they're trying to speak, but it is nice to have some reprieve from the barrage of COVID admissions.

A benefit of having the conference over video is that if I'm not on service or working that day, I can log in from my laptop while relaxing at my favorite spot at the gliderport, taking in the view while listening to the conference on my earbuds.

As I look at all the doctors through their webcams, I notice that most have subtle changes in demeanor. There is a degree of exhaustion from the taxing two years we've all had. But there also is a greater sense of appreciation. We still talk about science and medicine, but more and more, we're bringing up issues of meaning and purpose, both for our patients and for us.

Every now and then during Grand Rounds, one of the older docs will comment on how the culture of medicine has changed, largely for the better. Peering over worn, leather-bound notebooks, they reminisce about a time when patients would heed the warnings of their doctors with more enormity. Medicine has moved away from the classic paternalistic approach, where the physician tells the patient what is good for their health akin to how a parent would tell their child to eat their vegetables. The field has shifted to one of shared decision making as doctors and patients work together to make informed decisions about their health care that is in line with the patient's goals.

Nevertheless, some patients require active prompting from their physician, as we constantly remind them to schedule their annual physicals, screening colonoscopies, mammograms, and blood tests in a constant barrage of reminders that borders on nagging. Other patients require no reminders, always being on top of their health-care maintenance both inside the clinic and out. Among these, there is a subset of patients that strives to do everything in their power to retain their youthful health. In their desperation, they turn to unstudied supplements and experimental diets to stave off death. Like Gilgamesh on his journey for immortality, they plead for anything and everything to prolong their lives.

I'm still pretty early on in my career in medicine. But thus far, I have never had a patient escape death. Yet.

I've helped patients temporarily elude death. I've bought patients a few months or years at times. Some have died before I anticipated. Many have lived beyond the time I thought they had left. But every patient I've met has, or at some time will, die. In my experience, death does not care whether you are ready or not. It comes for everyone and rarely gives us a heads up or second chance.

Believe it or not, I knew that everyone dies before my first lecture in medical school. I suspect you did not need to read this book in order to know this simple fact. You also did not need to read this book to know that before that inevitable day comes, you will *live*.

Some of us have decades. Some of us have days. Some of us may know that death is coming for us, through a recent diagnosis of a terminal illness. Others of us are blessed with health and have not had death brought up on our radars.

The most heartbreaking are the cases where the individual's heart is still beating, but they have lost meaning and fulfillment in their life. Nineteenth century playwright and author Gertrude Nelson Andrews said, "There is no reason why a person shouldn't be young at eighty, but there are a whole lot of people who die at fifty and aren't buried until they are eighty."[162]

Regardless of how much time you have left, you can choose how you live your life until that point. Many of us have the privilege to control certain aspects of our lives. We can choose to pursue our passions. Dedicate ourselves to our families, communities, or causes.

And all of us can choose the mindset we bring to life.

The death that met, and in many cases took, the patients we got to know will also come for us. We will be faced with our own mortality, just as everyone you read about was. No matter how we attempt to elude death, just like Gilgamesh, we will have to accept our own mortality. It is better to do so earlier rather than later so that we can get as much *living* in as possible before then.

Dave Sackett, the father of evidence-based medicine, famously said, "Half of what you'll learn in medical school will be shown to be either dead wrong or out of date within five years of your graduation; the trouble is that nobody can tell you which half."[163]

Medical schools will use this quote to motivate students and faculty alike to continue to stay on the forefront of science.

I suspect the ratio of what we know about meaning, purpose, and fulfillment is even greater. But just as I will continue to keep up with the medicine, I will continue to learn from my patients so I can live with meaning, love, purpose, and kindness. So that when my time comes, I too can say I lived a fulfilling life.

Acknowledgments

This work began as a way for a newly minted physician thrust into the midst of the pandemic to find meaning amongst death and sickness. What was originally written as a personal journal of lessons and conversations would not have made it to its current form in your hands without some incredible individuals who provided encouragement when hope was in short supply. Any good I possess is a direct reflection of the lessons learned from the extraordinary people who inspire me to be better.

I am deeply grateful to my father, Aqil Abbasi, who leads a life of courage and principles and taught me the importance of holding steadfast to one's values, especially in the most challenging times. I strive daily to follow in your footsteps.

My mother, Attia Abbasi, the very reason I became a doctor, embodies unwavering dedication and compassion toward her patients. She pours her mind, heart, and soul into their care. To be even half the doctor she is would be a blessing beyond measure.

My awe-inspiring little sister, Javairia Abbasi, exemplifies the strength to be kind, even in the face of cruelty. She is my hero, a guiding light in my life.

To my dearest friend, Mariam Haq, who taught me the profound power of a warm heart, especially when the world feels coldest. She is the softness and warmth that fills my life.

My eternal gratitude to my grandparents: Dada Abu, Shaukat Abbas Abbasi, you showed me the magic in the written word. Dadi Ami, Mumtaz Jehan, you taught me what it means to truly care for family. Nana Abu, Muhammad Kazim Minhas, your unwavering work ethic inspires me still. Nani Ami, Haleema Begum, your gentle piety shaped my soul. Thank you for the gifts you've given me.

Our incredible community in Granite Bay, California nurtured me in the most loving and enriching environment imaginable.

My extended family in California, New York, and beyond have always showered me with boundless love and care. If it truly takes a village, I couldn't have asked for a more beautiful one to call my own.

My day-one friends Jibran Khan, Daniel Graham, Hammad Mahir, Aneeq Malik, Hasan Javed, and Haroon Ghori have been steadfast pillars of support. Thank you for your unwavering encouragement and friendship.

I extend my heartfelt gratitude to the amazing teachers within the Eureka Union School District, including the exceptional Doña Leeds, for their dedication and passion in shaping young minds.

I am grateful to Amer Metwalli for his unwavering support and guidance, which fostered an environment where I could explore and nurture my spiritual growth as a Muslim American.

The exceptional physicians at Scripps Clinic Medical Group exemplify the highest standards of patient care, regardless of the challenges. My deepest gratitude to the incredible physician faculty, including but not limited to Shazia Jamil, Duc Do, Laura Nicholson, Roger Yu, Derek Jones, Carrie Chun, Liesbet Joris-Quinton, Farhad Shadan, Ayanna Boyd-King, and Biraj Shah.

To my fellow residents at the Scripps Clinic Internal Medicine Residency, including Nihal Patel, Priya Reddy, Samuel Kung, and Robby Tickes, thank you for the camaraderie and shared experiences in the trenches.

My Dartmouth College professors, particularly Ronald Shaiko, Yorke Brown, Peter Tse, William North, and Misagh Parsa, instilled in me a lifelong passion for learning. The Tucker Foundation's spiritual mentors, including Nancy Vogele, Dawood Yasin, and Sharif Rosen, taught me that spirit and heart are just as important as brains.

My professors at Northwestern University Feinberg School of Medicine instilled in me not only the science of medicine but also the empathy essential to its practice. I am forever indebted to Jeffrey Fronza, Michelle Fletcher, and John Nicolas. I learned just as much from my classmates including Seth Williams, and Akash and Ankita Adhia.

To Christina Lee and James Thomas, thank you for entrusting me with the most fulfilling job imaginable. To my extraordinary colleagues at Palo Alto Medical Foundation, including world class physicians Larry Crane, Bill Cheng, Crystal Evey, Mundeep Chawla, Kevin Yee, Philip Lee, Mimi Blaurock, John Cunniff, Abren Belay, Sam Lada, Joyce Cho, Sumi Chari, Kahee Jo, Libby Trevathan, Yi-Chiun Wang, Kha Lai, Walter Cheng, Philip Young, Nicole Rimpel, Kelsey Smith, Elizabeth Arias, and Nancy Hua. I am continually inspired by the empathetic, diligent, and high-quality care you provide to our patients.

Finally, a heartfelt thank you to Amy Ashby and her colleagues at Warren Publishing for your exceptional editing and for sharing my passion for this work.

Endnotes

1 "COVID Data Tracker, Atlanta, GA," Center for Disease Control and Prevention, US Department of Health and Human Services, CDC, accessed July 23, 2022, https://covid.cdc.gov/COVID-data-tracker/#datatracker-home.

2 Gregory A. Roth et al., "Trends in Patient Characteristics and COVID-19 In-Hospital Mortality in the United States During the COVID-19 Pandemic," *JAMA Network Open* 4, no. 5 (May 2021), https://www.ncbi.nlm.nih.gov/pmc/articles/PMC8094014/.

3 Yi-Chun Chen, Hsien-Ching Chiu, and Chia-Yu Chu, "Drug Reaction With Eosinophilia and Systemic Symptoms: A Retrospective Study of 60 Cases," *Arch Dermatol* 146, no. 12 (August 2010): 1373–1379, https://jamanetwork.com/journals/jamadermatology/fullarticle/422535.

4 Stelios Kiosses, *The Power of Talking: Stories from the Therapy Room* (Manila: Phoenix Publishing House, 2021).

5 Leonard L. Martin, W. Keith Campbell, and Christopher D. Henry, "The Roar of Awakening: Mortality Acknowledgment as a Call to Authentic Living," in *Handbook of Experimental Existential Psychology*, ed. J. Greenberg, S. L. Koole, & T. Pyszczynski, (New York: Guilford Press, 2004), 431–448.

6 Larry Rosenberg, "The Supreme Meditation," *Lion's Roar*, (September 15, 2020), https://www.lionsroar.com/the-supreme-meditation/.

7 Tim J. Winter, "The Muslim grand narrative," in *Caring for Muslim Patients* (Oxfordshire: Routledge Publishing Ltd, 2021), 25–34.

8 Sunan Ibn Majah, Vol. 5, Book of Zuhd, Hadith 4259.

9 Lucius Annaeus Seneca, *On the Shortness of Life*, Vol. 1 (London: Penguin UK, 2004).

10 Institute of Medicine, *Strategies to Improve Cardiac Arrest Survival: A Time to Act*, (Washington DC: The National Academies Press, 2015), https://doi.org/10.17226/21723.

11 "CPR Facts & Status," CPR & First Aid Emergency Cardiovascular Care, American Heart Association, https://cpr.heart.org/en/resources/cpr-facts-and-stats.

12 Thomas W. Zoch et al., "Short- and Long-term Survival After Cardiopulmonary Resuscitation," *Arch Intern Med.* 160, no. 13 (January 6, 2000): 1969–1973. https://jamanetwork.com/journals/jamainternalmedicine/fullarticle/485389.

13 Melikşah Demir, Ömer Faruk Şimşek, and Amanda D. Procsal, "I Am so Happy 'Cause My Best Friend Makes Me Feel Unique: Friendship, Personal Sense of Uniqueness and Happiness," *Journal of Happiness Studies* 14, no. 4 (2013): 1201–1224, https://doi.org/10.1007/s10902-012-9376-9.

14 Ed Diener and Martin E.P. Seligman, "Very Happy People," *Psychological Science* 13, no. 1 (January 2002): 81-84, https://doi.org/10.1111/1467-9280.00415.

15 Robert M. Seyfarth and Dorothy L. Cheney, "The Evolutionary Origins of Friendship," *Annual Review of Psychology* 63, (July 5, 2011): 153–177, https://pubmed.ncbi.nlm.nih.gov/21740224/.

16 Nicole K. Valtora, et al., "Loneliness and social isolation as risk factors for coronary heart disease and stroke: systematic review and meta-analysis of longitudinal observational studies," *Heart* 102, no. 13 (April 18, 2016): 1009–1016, https://pubmed.ncbi.nlm.nih.gov/27091846/.

17 Julianne Holt-Lunstad et al., "Loneliness and Social Isolation as Risk Factors for Mortality: A Meta-Analytic Review," *Perspectives on Psychological Science* 10, no. 2, (March 2015): 227–237, https://pubmed.ncbi.nlm.nih.gov/25910392/.

18 Julianne Holt-Lunstad, "The Potential Public Health Relevance of Social Isolation and Loneliness: Prevalence, Epidemiology, and Risk Factors," *Public Policy & Aging Report* 27, no. 4 (January 2, 2018): 127–130, https://academic.oup.com/ppar/article/27/4/127/4782506.

19 N. Leigh-Hunt et al., "An overview of systematic reviews on the public health consequences of social isolation and loneliness," *Public Health* 152, (September 12, 2017): 157–171, https://pubmed.ncbi.nlm.nih.gov/28915435/.

20 Jill L. Guttormson et al., "Critical Care Nurse Burnout, Moral Distress, and Mental Health During the COVID-19 Pandemic: A United States Survey," *Heart Lung* 55, (September/October 2022): 127–133, https://www.ncbi.nlm.nih.gov/pmc/articles/PMC9050623/.

21 Prem S. Fry, and Dominique L. Debats, "Perfectionism and the Five-Factor Personality Traits as Predictors of Mortality in Older Adults," *Journal of Health Psychology* 14, no. 4 (May 2009): 513–524, https://pubmed.ncbi.nlm.nih.gov/19383652/.

22 Madeleine Ferari et al., "Self-compassion moderates the perfectionism and depression link in both adolescence and adulthood," *PLOS One* 13, no. 2 (February 21 2018), https://www.ncbi.nlm.nih.gov/pmc/articles/PMC5821438/.

23 Glenn R. Fox et al., "Neural correlates of gratitude," *Frontiers in Psychology* 6, (September 30, 2015): 1491, https://www.ncbi.nlm.nih.gov/pmc/articles/PMC4588123/.

24 Andrew Huberman, "The Science of Gratitude & How to Build a Gratitude Practice," November 22, 2021, YouTube video, 1:25:56, https://www.youtube.com/watch?v=KVjfFN89qvQ.

25 Jeffrey J. Froh, William J. Sefick, and Robert A. Emmons, "Counting blessings in early adolescents: An experimental study of gratitude and subjective well-being," *Journal of School Psychology* 46, no. 2 (2008): 213–233, https://greatergood.berkeley.edu/pdfs/GratitudePDFs/3Froh-BlessingsEarlyAdolescence.pdf.

26 Nathaniel M. Lambert et al., "Benefits of Expressing Gratitude: Expressing Gratitude to a Partner Changes One's View of the Relationship," *Psychological Science* 21, no. 4 (April, 21, 2010): 574–580, https://pubmed.ncbi.nlm.nih.gov/20424104/.

27 Alex M. Wood, Stephen Joseph, and John Maltby, "Gratitude predicts psychological well-being above the Big Five facets," *Personality and Individual Differences* 46, no. 4 (March 2009): 443–447, https://www.sciencedirect.com/science/article/abs/pii/S019188690800425X.

28 Todd B. Kashdan, Gitendra Uswatte, and Terri Julian, "Gratitude and hedonic and eudaimonic well-being in Vietnam war veterans," *Behavior Research and Therapy* 44, no. 2 (February 2006): 177–199, https://pubmed.ncbi.nlm.nih.gov/16389060/.

29 Sunghyon Kyeong et al., "Effects of gratitude meditation on neural network functional connectivity and brain-heart coupling," *Scientific Reports* 7, no. 1 (July 11, 2017): 1–15, https://pubmed.ncbi.nlm.nih.gov/28698643/.

30 Laura I. Hazlett et al., "Exploring neural mechanisms of the health benefits of gratitude in women: A randomized controlled trial," *Brain, Behavior, and Immunity* 95, (July 2021): 444–453, https://www.sciencedirect.com/science/article/pii/S0889159121001177X.

31 Matteo Cesari, et al., "Inflammatory Markers and Onset of Cardiovascular Events: Results From the Health ABC study," *Circulation* 108, no. 19 (November 11, 2003): 2317–2322, https://pubmed.ncbi.nlm.nih.gov/14568895/.

32 Rikke Krogh-Madsen et al., "Influence of TNF-*a* and IL-6 infusions on insulin sensitivity and expression of IL-18 in humans," *American Journal of Physiology-Endocrinology and Metabolism* 291, no. 1 (July 29, 2006): 108–114, https://pubmed.ncbi.nlm.nih.gov/16464907/#:~:text=TNF%20induced%20IL%2D18%20gene,gene%20expression%20in%20either%20tissue.

33 Yi Ren Yungfeng Ma et al., "IL-6, IL-8 and TNF-*a* levels correlate with disease stage in breast cancer patients," *Advances in Clinical and Experimental Medicine* 26, no. 3 (May/June 2017): 421–426, https://pubmed.ncbi.nlm.nih.gov/28791816/.

34 Amit Kumar and Nicholas Epley, "Undervaluing Gratitude: Expressers Misunderstand the Consequences of Showing Appreciation," *Psychological Science* 29, no. 9 (June 2018): 1423–1435, https://www.researchgate.net/publication/326022743_Undervaluing_Gratitude_Expressers_Misunderstand_the_Consequences_of_Showing_Appreciation.

35 Hongbo Yu et al., "Neural substrates and social consequences of interpersonal gratitude: Intention matters," *Emotion* 17, no. 4 (June 2017): 589, https://pubmed.ncbi.nlm.nih.gov/27936814/.

36 Martin J. Tobin and Karl Yang, "Weaning from Mechanical Ventilation," *Critical Care Clinics* 6, no. 3 (July 1990): 725–747.

37 Niall McCrae, Sheryl Gettings, and Edward Purssell, "Social Media and Depressive Symptoms in Childhood and Adolescence: A Systematic Review," *Adolescent Research Review* 2, no. 4 (March 2, 2017): 315–330, https://link.springer.com/article/10.1007/s40894-017-0053-4.

38 "New victims from Pompeii emerge from the excavation of the House of the Chaste Lovers," Pompeii (website), Accessed July 7, 2023, http://pompeiisites.org/en/comunicati/new-victims-from-pompeii-emerge-from-the-excavation-of-the-house-of-the-chaste-lovers/.

39 Debra Umberson, "Gender, marital status and the social control of health behavior," *Social Science & Medicine* 34, no. 8 (April 1992): 907–917, https://pubmed.ncbi.nlm.nih.gov/1604380/.

40 Robert P. Murray et al., "Social support for smoking cessation and abstinence: The lung health study," *Addictive Behaviors* 20, no. 2 (March/April 1995): 159–170, https://pubmed. ncbi.nlm.nih.gov/7484310/.

41 Janice K. Kiecolt-Glaser and Tamara L. Newton, "Marriage and health: His and hers," *Psychological Bulletin* 127, no. 4 (July 2001): 472, https://pubmed.ncbi.nlm.nih.gov/11439708/.

42 Robin J.H. Russell and Pamela A. Wells, "Predictors of happiness in married couples," *Personality and Individual Differences* 17, no. 3 (September 1994): 313–321, https://doi. org/10.1016/0191-8869(94)90279-8.

43 Sheetal Yadav and S.K. Srivastava, "A study of marital satisfaction and happiness among love married couples and arrange married couples," *International Review of Social Sciences and Humanities* 9, no. 8 (August 2019): 1–9, https://doi.org/10.1016/j.ssresearch.2012.09.002.

44 Shawn Grover and John F. Helliwell, "How's Life at Home? New Evidence on Marriage and the Set Point for Happiness," *Journal of Happiness Studies: An Interdisciplinary Forum on Subjective Well-Being* 20, no. 2 (February 15, 2019): 373–390, https://doi.org/10.1007/s10902-017-9941-3.

45 Muhammad I. Tirmidhi, *Jami' Al-Tirmidhi*, (Karachi: Karkhana Tijarat Kutab, 1900).

46 *Plato, The Symposium,* trans. Frisbee C.C. Sheffield (Cambridge: Cambridge University Press, 2008).

47 Simone De Beauvoir, *The Second Sex* (New York: Knopf, 2010).

48 Simone De Beauvoir, *She Came to Stay: A Novel* (New York: W W Norton & Company, 1999).

49 Ingeborg Alexandersen et al., "'I want to get back!' A qualitative study of long-term critically ill patients' inner strength and willpower: Back home after long-term intensive care," *Journal of Clinical Nursing* 30, no. 19–20 (October 2021): 3023–3035, https://pubmed.ncbi.nlm.nih. gov/34018274/.

50 Katharina Bernecker and Veronika Job, "Beliefs About Willpower Are Related to Therapy Adherence and Psychological Adjustment in Patients With Type 2 Diabetes," *Basic and Applied Social Psychology* 37, no. 3 (2015): 188–195, https://doi.org/10.1080/01973533.2015.1049348.

51 G. Antiliou, L. Timotijevic, and M. Raats, "The role of willpower in successful maintenance of weight loss," *Psychology & Health* 27, (August 21-25, 2012): 148–149, https://openresearch.surrey.ac.uk/esploro/outputs/99516412102346?institution=44SUR_ INST&skipUsageReporting=true&recordUsage=false.

52 Angela Lee Duckworth and Patrick D. Quinn, "Development and Validation of the Short Grit Scale (Grit-S)," *Journal of Personality Assessment* 91, no. 2 (February 10, 2009): 166–174, https://doi.org/10.1080/00223890802634290.

53 Veronika Job et al., "Implicit theories about willpower predict self-regulation and grades in everyday life," *Journal of Personality and Social Psychology* 108, no. 4 (2015): 637–647, https:// doi.org/10.1037/pspp0000014.

54 E.M. Camacho, S.M.M. Verstappen, and D.P.M. Symmons "Association between socioeconomic status, learned helplessness, and disease outcome in patients with inflammatory polyarthritis," *Arthritis Care & Research* 64, no. 8 (March 21, 2012): 1225–1232, https://doi. org/10.1002/acr.21677.

55 Mac Anderson, *Power of Attitude* (Naperville, Ill: Sourcebooks, Inc., 2005).

56 Kris R. Henning and B. Christopher Frueh, "Combat guilt and its relationship to PTSD symptoms," *Journal of Clinical Psychology* 53, no. 8 (December 8, 1997): 801–808, https://doi.org/10.1002/(SICI)1097-4679(199712)53:8<801::AID-JCLP3>3.0.CO;2-I.

57 J.K. Foster, G.A. Eskes, and D.T. Stuss, "The cognitive neuropsychology of attention: A frontal lobe perspective," *Cognitive Neuropsychology* 11, no. 2 (1994): 133–147, https://doi.org/10.1080/02643299408251971.

58 T. Hanninen et al., "Decline of Frontal Lobe Functions in Subjects with Age-associated Memory Impairment," *Neurology* 48, no. 1 (January 1, 1997): 148–153, https://doi.org/10.1212/WNL.48.1.148.

59 Kelseyleigh Reber, *If I Fall* (New York: Aperture Press, 2013).

60 Vicki D. Lachman, "Moral courage: a virtue in need of development?," *MedSurg Nursing* 16, no. 2 (April 2007): 131, https://go.gale.com/ps/i.do?id=GALE%7CA163422064&sid=googleScholar&v=2.1&it=r&linkaccess=abs&issn=10920811&p=AONE&sw=w&userGroupName=anon%7E3fbacf26&aty=open-web-entry.

61 Al Gini, "A Short Primer on Moral Courage," in Moral Courage in Organizations: Doing the Right Thing at Work, eds. Debra Comer and Gina Vega (New York: Routledge, 2015), 27–36.

62 John Zumbrunnen, "'Courage in the Face of Reality': Nietzsche's Admiration for Thucydides," *Polity* 35, no. 2 (2002): 237–263, https://www.journals.uchicago.edu/doi/abs/10.1086/POLv35n2ms3235499#:~:text=Abstract,explore%20Nietzsche's%20admiration%20for%20Thucydides.

63 Sean T. Hannah, Bruce J. Avolio, and Fred O. Walumbwa, "Relationships between Authentic Leadership, Moral Courage, and Ethical and Pro-Social Behaviors," *Business Ethics Quarterly* 21, no. 4 (October 2011): 555-578, https://doi.org/10.5840/beq201121436.

64 Susan M. Gallagher, "Bullying, Moral Courage, Patient Safety, and the Bariatric Nurse," *Bariatric Nursing and Surgical Patient Care* 7, no. 4 (December 2012): 156–159, https://doi.org/10.1089/bar.2012.9954.

65 Michael Greenstone and Vishan Nigam, "Does Social Distancing Matter?" (working paper, University of Chicago, Baker Friedman Institute for Economics, 2020), https://bfi.uchicago.edu/wp-content/uploads/BFI_WP_202026.pdf.

66 David Christensen, Jeff Barnes, and David Rees, "Developing Resolve to Have Moral Courage: A Field Comparison of Teaching Methods," *Journal of Business Ethics Education* 4, (2007): 79–96, https://www.proquest.com/openview/4a2d8ca54a50b5b2ea29ebd181515d0d/1?pq-origsite=gscholar&cbl=307110.

67 Martin Luther King Jr, "Remaining Awake Through A Great Revolution" (speech), A.M.E. Church Convention, May 8th, 1964, Cincinnati, OH, (Creed Records, 1971).

68 Suzy Kassem, *Rise Up and Salute the Sun: The Writings of Suzy Kassem* (Sedona: Awakened Press, 2011).

69 Kees van den Bos, "Meaning making following activation of the behavioral inhibition system: How caring less about what others think may help us to make sense of what is going on," in *The Psychology of Meaning*, eds. K.D. Markman, T. Proulx, and M.J. Lindberg (Washington DC, American Psychological Association, 2013), 359-380, https://doi.org/10.1037/14040-018.

70 Seneca, "Letter 52," in *Moral Letters to Lucilius*, trans. Richard Mott Gummere (London: William Heinemann, 1917/1920/1925), https://en.wikisource.org/wiki/Moral_letters_to_Lucilius/Letter_52

71 Carl Gustav Jung, "Archaic Man," in *Modern Man in Search of a Soul* (New York: Routledge, 2001), 137–164.

72 Richard E. Boettcher, "Interspousal Empathy, Marital Satisfaction, and Marriage Counseling," *Journal of Social Service Research* 1, no. 1 (1977): 105-113, https://doi.org/10.1300/J079v01n01_08.

73 Zarghuna Naseem and Ruhi Khalid, "Positive Thinking in Coping with Stress and Health Outcomes: Literature Review," *Journal of Research & Reflections in Education (JRRE)* 4, no. 1 (2010), https://www.semanticscholar.org/paper/Positive-Thinking-in-Coping-with-Stress-and-Health-Naseem-Khalid/db77200dc777353a922594e868554b12e0c8448b.

74 Gabriele Oettingen and Thomas A. Wadden, "Expectation, fantasy, and weight loss: Is the impact of positive thinking always positive?," *Cognitive Therapy and Research* 15, no. 2 (1991): 167–175, https://doi.org/10.1007/BF01173206.

75 M.J.C. Forgeard and M.E.P. Seligman, "Seeing the glass half full: A review of the causes and consequences of optimism," *Pratiques Psychologiques* 18, no. 2 (June 2012): 107–120, https://doi.org/10.1016/j.prps.2012.02.002.

76 Henriette Engberg et al., "Optimism and survival: does an optimistic outlook predict better survival at advanced ages? A twelve-year follow-up of Danish nonagenarians," *Aging Clinical and Experimental Research* 25, no. 5 (September 7, 2013): 517–525, https://doi.org/10.1007/s40520-013-0122-x.

77 Jonas Preposi Cruz et al., "Optimism, proactive coping and quality of life among nurses: A cross-sectional study," *Journal of Clinical Nursing* 27, no. 9–10 (March 30, 2018): 2098–2108, https://doi.org/10.1111/jocn.14363.

78 Feng Jiang et al., "How Belief in a Just World Benefits Mental Health: The Effects of Optimism and Gratitude," *Social Indicators Research* 126, no. 1 (March 2016): 411–423, https://doi.org/10.1007/s11205-015-0877-x.

79 Ralph Waldo Emerson, *Success, Greatness, Immortality* (Boston: Houghton, Osgood and Company, 1880).

80 May Sarton, *Journal of a Solitude* (New York: W.W. Norton & Company, 1992).

81 Bruce Eamon Brown, *1001 Motivational Messages and Quotes for Athletes and Coaches: Teaching Character Through Sport* (Monterey, CA: Coaches Choice, 2000).

82 Charles Johnston, *From the Upanishads* (Portland, ME: Thomas B. Mosher, 1913).

83 Ezekiel 36:25 (ESV), https://biblehub.com/ezekiel/36-25.htm.

84 Quran, 21–30.

85 Danny Chau, "What It Means to Understand Bruce Lee," *The Atlantic*, June 22, 2020, https://www.theatlantic.com/culture/archive/2020/06/be-water-and-difficulty-understanding-bruce-lee/613234/.

86 Steven Solomon, *Water: The Epic Struggle for Wealth, Power, and Civilization* (New York: HarperCollins, 2010).

87 Sue Waite, "'Memories are made of this': Some reflections on outdoor learning and recall," *Education 3-13* 35, no. 4 (2007): 333–347, https://doi.org/10.1080/03004270701602459.

88 Gwang-Won Kim, et al., "Functional Neuroanatomy Associated with Natural and Urban Scenic Views in the Human Brain: 3.0 T Functional MR Imaging," *Korean Journal of Radiology* 11, no. 5 (August, 27, 2010): 507–513, https://doi.org/10.3348/kjr.2010.11.5.507.

89 Wallace J. Nichols, *Blue Mind: The Surprising Science that Shows how Being Near, In, On, or Under Water Can Make You Happier, Healthier, More Connected, and Better at What You Do* (Boston: Little, Brown and Company, 2014).

90 Byoung-Suk Kweon et al., "Anger and Stress: The Role of Landscape Posters in an Office Setting," *Environment and Behavior* 40, no. 3 (2007): 355–381, https://doi.org/10.1177/0013916506298797.

91 Amelia Elena Stan, "Psychological effects of aquatic activity in hydrotherapy programs," *Marathon* 5, no. 2 (2013): 205–209, https://doi.org/10.3389/fpsyt.2022.1051551.

92 Caterina McEvoy, "Blue Dragon, White Tiger: The Paradox of Flux and Flow in Sound Art and Martial Arts" (PhD diss., University of Sheffield, 2019), https://etheses.whiterose.ac.uk/25751/1/PhD_Caterina%20McEvoy_Final%20Thesis%202020.pdf.

93 Kassem, *Rise Up and Salute the Sun: The Writings of Suzy Kassem.*

94 Simon Gay, "Together, we are an ocean," *Education for Primary Care* 33, no. 1 (November, 22, 2021): 1, https://doi.org/10.1080/14739879.2021.2005469.

95 Loretta J. Ross, "Speaking up without tearing down," *Learning for Justice* 61, *(Spring 2019),* https://www.learningforjustice.org/magazine/spring-2019/speaking-up-without-tearing-down.

96 Katherine D. Kinzler and Elizabeth S. Spelke, "Do infants show social preferences for people differing in race?," *Cognition* 119, no. 1 (April 2011): 1–9, https://doi.org/10.1016/j.cognition.2010.10.019.

97 Steven O. Roberts and Michael T. Rizzo, "The Psychology of American Racism," *American Psychologist* 76, no. 3 (2021): 475, doi: 10.1037/amp0000642.

98 Denise M. Bostdorff, "The internet rhetoric of the Ku Klux Klan: A case study in web site community building run amok," *Communication Studies* 55, no. 2 (2004): 340–361, https://doi.org/10.1080/10510970409388623.

99 Timothy J. Madigan and Daria Gorlova, "Aristotle on Forming Friendships," *Philosophy Now* 126, (2018): 6, https://philosophynow.org/issues/126/Aristotle_on_Forming_Friendships#:~:text=For%20Aristotle%2C%20friendships%2C%20especially%20friendships,should%20not%20be%20given%20lightly.

100 Aristotle, *Nicomachean Ethics* (Indianapolis: Hackett Publishing, 2019).

101 Kristen D. Neff, Kristen L. Kirkpatrick, and Stephanie S. Rude, "Self-compassion and adaptive psychological functioning," *Journal of Research in Personality* 41, no. 1 (2007): 139–154, https://doi.org/10.1016/j.jrp.2006.03.004.

102 Kristen D. Neff, Stephanie S. Rude, and Kristen L. Kirkpatrick, "An examination of self-compassion in relation to positive psychological functioning and personality traits," *Journal of Research in Personality* 41, no. 4 (2007): 908–916, doi:10.1016/j.jrp.2006.08.002.

103 Jean M. Twenge, *Generation Me—Revised and Updated: Why Today's Young Americans are More Confident, Assertive, Entitled—and More Miserable Than Ever Before,* (New York: Simon & Schuster, 2014).

104 Kristen Neff, "The Space Between Self-Esteem and Self-Compassion," February 6, 2013, TEDx Centennial Park Women, YouTube video, 19:00, https://www.youtube.com/watch?v=IvtZBUSplr4.

105 Ricks Warren, Elke Smeets, and Kristen Neff, "Self-criticism and self-compassion: risk and resilience: Being compassionate to oneself is associated with emotional resilience and psychological well-being," *Current Psychiatry* 15, no. 12 (December 2016): 18–28, https://self-compassion.org/wp-content/uploads/2016/12/Self-Criticism.pdf.

106 Jennifer Katz and Rebecca A. Nelson, "Family Experiences and Self-Criticism in College Students: Testing a Model of Family Stress, Past Unfairness, and Self-Esteem," *The American Journal of Family Therapy* 35, no. 5 (October 3, 2007): 447–457, https://doi.org/10.1080/01926180601057630.

107 Kevin P. Young et al., "Health Care Workers' Mental Health and Quality of Life During COVID-19: Results From a Mid-Pandemic, National Survey," *Psychiatric Services* 72, no. 2 (December 3, 2020): 122–128, https://doi.org/10.1176/appi.ps.202000424.

108 Shijiao Yan et al., "The global survival rate among adult out-of-hospital cardiac arrest patients who received cardiopulmonary resuscitation: A systematic review and meta-analysis," *Critical Care* 24, no. 61 (February 22, 2020), https://doi.org/10.1186/s13054-020-2773-2.

109 Jennifer Setlack, "Workplace Violence and Mental Health of Paramedics and Firefighters," (Master's thesis, University of Manitoba, 2019), https://mspace.lib.umanitoba.ca/items/149f5c7c-c8d3-4a01-8ed8-cd3e4bcfbe6c.

110 Kristen D. Neff, "Self-Compassion, Self-Esteem, and Well-Being," *Social and Personality Psychology Compass* 5, no. 1 (January 4, 2011): 1–12, https://doi.org/10.1111/j.1751-9004.2010.00330.x.

111 Alexander H. Jordan et al., "Misery Has More Company Than People Think: Underestimating the Prevalence of Others' Negative Emotions," *Personality and Social Psychology Bulletin* 37, no. 1 (December 22, 2010): 120–135, https://doi.org/10.1177/0146167210390822.

112 Kristen D. Neff and Katie A. Dahm, "Self-Compassion: What It Is, What It Does, and How It Relates To Mindfulness," in *Handbook of Mindfulness and Self-Regulation* (New York: Springer, 2015): 121–137.

113 Kasey Lloyd and William Pennington, "Towards a Theory of Minimalism and Wellbeing," *International Journal of Applied Positive Psychology* 5, no. 3 (2020): 121–136, https://doi.org/10.1007/s41042-020-00030-y.

114 Emma Bruehlman-Senecal and Ozlem Ayduk, "This too shall pass: temporal distance and the regulation of emotional distress," *Journal of Personality and Social Psychology* 108, no. 2 (February 2015): 356, https://doi.org/10.1037/a0038324.

115 Tessa M. Benson-Greenwald, "The Light at the End of the Tunnel: Temporal Distancing and Academic Attitudes," (PhD diss., Miami University, 2018).

116 Yuta Chishima, I-Ting Huai-Ching Liu, and Anne E. Wilson, "Temporal distancing during the COVID-19 pandemic: Letter writing with future self can mitigate negative affect," *Applied Psychology: Health and Well-Being* 13, no. 2 (May 2021): 406–418, https://doi.org/10.1111/aphw.12256.

117 James M. Rippe, "Lifestyle Medicine: The Health Promoting Power of Daily Habits and Practices," *American Journal of Lifestyle Medicine* 12, no. 6 (November/December 2018): 499–512, https://doi.org/10.1177/1559827618785554.

118 Shawn T. McClean et al., "Stumbling out of the gate: The energy-based implications of morning routine disruption," *Personnel Psychology* 74, no. 3 (2021): 411–448, https://doi.org/10.1111/peps.12419.

119 Admiral William H. McRaven, *Make Your Bed: Little Things that Can Change Your Life ... and Maybe the World* (London: Hachette UK, 2017).

120 Christopher Hansen-Barkun, et al., "Personal protective equipment portraits in the era of COVID-19," *European Journal of Internal Medicine* 102, (May 2022): 125–127, https://doi.org/10.1016/j.ejim.2022.05.026.

121 Sigal G. Barsade, "The Ripple Effect: Emotional Contagion and its Influence on Group Behavior," *Administrative Science Quarterly* 47, no. 4 (December 2002): 644–675, https://doi.org/10.2307/3094912.

122 Cassie Mogilner and Michael I. Norton, "Time, money, and happiness," *Current Opinion in Psychology* 10, (2016): 12-16, https://www.hbs.edu/ris/Publication%20Files/mogilner%20norton%202016_951db108-1099-4482-8b02-27eed5e2a87e.pdf.

123 Montaigne, "Of Repentance," in *The Complete Essays of Montaigne*, ed. and trans. Donald M. Frame (Redwood City, CA: Stanford University Press, 1957), 614.

124 Elizabeth Page-Gould, "The Unhealthy Racist," in *Are We Born Racist?*, eds. Jason Marsh, Roldolfo Mendoza-Denton, and Jeremy Adam Smith (Boston: Beacon Press, 2010), 41–44.

125 Elizabeth Page-Gould et al., "Understanding the impact of cross-group friendship on interactions with novel outgroup members," *Journal of Personality and Social Psychology* 98, no. 5 (May 2010): 775.

126 Wendy Berry Mendes et al., "Challenge and Threat During Social Interactions With White and Black Men," *Personality and Social Psychology Bulletin* 28, no. 7 (July 2002): 939–952, https://doi.org/10.1177/014616720202800707.

127 Brett W. Pelham and William B. Swann, "From self-conceptions to self-worth: On the sources and structure of global self-esteem," *Journal of Personality and Social Psychology* 57, no.4 (1989): 672.

128 John M. Chamberlain and David A.F. Haaga, "Unconditional Self-Acceptance and Responses to Negative Feedback," *Journal of Rational-Emotive & Cognitive-Behavior Therapy* 19, no. 3 (September 2001): 177–189, https://doi.org/10.1023/A:1011141500670.

129 Brian L. Thompson and Jennifer A. Waltz, "Mindfulness, self-esteem, and unconditional self-acceptance," *Journal of Rational-Emotive & Cognitive-Behavior Therapy* 26, no. 2 (2008): 119–126, https://doi.org/10.1007/s10942-007-0059-0.

130 Camilla S. Øverup et al. "I know I have to earn your love: how the family environment shapes feelings of worthiness of love," *International Journal of Adolescence and Youth* 22, no. 1 (January 28, 2014): 16–35, https://doi.org/10.1080/02673843.2013.868362.

131 Brené Brown, *Braving the Wilderness: The Quest for True Belonging and the Courage to Stand Alone* (New York: Random House, 2017).

132 Mihaly Csikszentmihalyi, *Flow: The Psychology of Optimal Experience* (New York: Harper and Row, 1990).

133 Steven Kotler, *The Rise of Superman: Decoding the Science of Ultimate Human Performance* (Boston: Houghton Mifflin Harcourt).

134 C. Heine, "Flow and achievement in mathematics," (Unpublished PhD diss., University of Chicago, 1996).

135 Jawaid A. Ghani and Satish P. Deshpande, "Task Characteristics and the Experience of Optimal Flow in Human—Computer Interaction," *The Journal of Psychology* 128, no. 4 (1994): 381–391.

136 Arnold B. Bakker, "Flow among music teachers and their students: The crossover of peak experiences," *Journal of Vocational Behavior* 66, no.1 (February 2005): 26–44, https://doi.org/10.1016/j.jvb.2003.11.001.

137 Cameron Norsworthy, Paul Gorczynski, and Susan A. Jackson, "A systematic review of flow training on flow states and performance in elite athletes," *Graduate Journal of Sport, Exercise & Physical Education Research* 6, no. 2 (2017): 16–28, https://www.researchgate.net/profile/Cameron-Norsworthy/publication/322676172_A_SYSTEMATIC_REVIEW_OF_FLOW_TRAINING_ON_FLOW_STATES_AND_PERFORMANCE_IN_ELITE_ATHLETES/links/5e6726b5a6fdcc37dd15e0e0/A-SYSTEMATIC-REVIEW-OF-FLOW-TRAINING-ON-FLOW-STATES-AND-PERFORMANCE-IN-ELITE-ATHLETES.pdf.

138 Csikszentmihalyi, *Flow: The Psychology of Optimal Experience* (New York: Harper and Row, 1990).

139 Lynn Marie Boianelli, "Achieving flow in theatre performance," (Master's thesis, Rowan University, September 2, 2005), https://rdw.rowan.edu/cgi/viewcontent.cgi?article=2907&context=etd.

140 Aliraza Aghababa and Ali Kashi, "Effect of mindful meditation on the mindfulness state, flow and sport performance," *Sport Psychology Studies* 7, no. 25 (2018): 89–110, https://doi.org/10.22089/spsyj.2018.5898.1626.

141 Jai Paul Dudeja, "Scientific Analysis of Mantra-Based Meditation and its Beneficial Effects: An Overview," *International Journal of Advanced Scientific Technologies in Engineering and Management Sciences* 3, no. 6 (June 2017): 21–26, http://www.ijastems.org/wp-content/uploads/2017/06/v3.i6.5.Scientific-Analysis-of-Mantra-Based-Meditation.pdf.

142 Helané Wahbeh et al., "A Systematic Review of Transcendent States Across Meditation and Contemplative Traditions," *Explore* 14, no. 1 (January/February 2018): 19–35, https://doi.org/10.1016/j.explore.2017.07.007.

143 Roberta Maeran and Francesco Cangiano, "Flow experience and job characteristics: Analyzing the role of flow in job satisfaction," *TPM-Testing, Psychometrics, Methodology in Applied Psychology* 20, no. 1 (2013): 13–26, https://psycnet.apa.org/record/2013-14149-002.

144 Amparo Castillo-Richmond et al., "Effects of Stress Reduction on Carotid Atherosclerosis in Hypertensive African Americans," *Stroke* 31, no. 3 (March 1, 2000): 568–573, https://doi.org/10.1161/01.STR.31.3.568.

145 Kenneth G. Walton et al., "Lowering Cortisol and CVD Risk in Postmenopausal Women: A Pilot Study Using the Transcendental Meditation Program," *Annals of the New York Academy of Sciences* 1032, no. 1 (December 2004): 211–215, https://doi.org/10.1196/annals.1314.023.

146 Mevlana Jalauddin Rumi, *Love's Ripening: Rumi on the Heart's Journey* (Boulder: Shambhala Publications, 2008).

147 Bruce Greyson, "Varieties of Near-Death Experience," *Psychiatry* 56, no. 4 (November 1993): 390–399, https://med.virginia.edu/perceptual-studies/wp-content/uploads/sites/360/2017/01/NDE25.pdf.

148 Sam Parnia, Ken Spearpoint, and Peter B. Fenwick, "Near death experiences, cognitive function and psychological outcomes of surviving cardiac arrest," *Resuscitation* 74, no. 2 (August 2007): 215–221,

149 Allan Kellehear, "Culture, Biology, and the Near-Death Experience: A Reappraisal," *Journal of Nervous and Mental Disease* 181, no. 3 (March 1993): 148–156, https://journals.lww.com/jonmd/abstract/1993/03000/culture,_biology,_and_the_near_death_experience__a.2.aspx.

150 J. E. Owens, Emily W. Cook, and Ian Stevenson, "Features of 'near-death experience' in relation to whether or not patients were near death," *The Lancet* 336, no. 8724 (November 10, 1990): 1175–1177, https://doi.org/10.1016/0140-6736(90)92780-L.

151 Sam Parnia and Peter Fenwick, "Near death experiences in cardiac arrest: visions of a dying brain or visions of a new science of consciousness," *Resuscitation* 52, no. 1 (January 2002): 5–11, https://doi.org/10.1016/S0300-9572(01)00469-5.

152 Van Lommel P., et al., "The Merkawah Research on Near Death Experience: A prospective study of 344 survivors of cardiac arrest," *The Lancet* (2001).

153 David Nutt and Robin Carhart-Harris, "The Current Status of Psychedelics in Psychiatry," *JAMA Psychiatry* 78, no. 2 (2021): 121–122, doi:10.1001/jamapsychiatry.2020.2171.

154 Rainer Kraehenmann et al., "Psilocybin-Induced Decrease in Amygdala Reactivity Correlates with Enhanced Positive Mood in Healthy Volunteers," *Biological Psychiatry* 78, no. 8 (October 2015): 572–581, https://doi.org/10.1016/j.biopsych.2014.04.010.

155 Robin L. Carhart-Harris et al., "Psilocybin for treatment-resistant depression: fMRI-measured brain mechanisms," *Scientific Reports* 7, no. 1 (October 13, 2017): 1–11, https://doi.org/10.1038/s41598-017-13282-7.

156 Susan Ling et al., "Molecular Mechanisms of Psilocybin and Implications for the Treatment of Depression," *CNS Drugs* 36, (November 17, 2021): 1–4, https://doi.org/10.1007/s40263-021-00877-y.

157 S. Ross et al., "Psychedelic-assisted psychotherapy to treat psychiatric and existential distress in life-threatening medical illnesses and palliative care," *Neuropharmacology* 216, (September 15, 2022): 109174, https://doi.org/10.1016/j.neuropharm.2022.109174.

158 Paul T.P. Wong, "Meaning management theory and death acceptance," in *Existential and Spiritual Issues in Death Attitudes* (New York: Psychology Press, 2007), 91–114, https://www.taylorfrancis.com/chapters/edit/10.4324/9780203809679-10/meaning-management-theory-death-acceptance-paul-wong.

159 Abraham Harold Maslow, "Dynamics of personality organization. I.," *Psychological Review* 50, no. 5 (1943): 514, https://doi.org/10.1037/h0062222.

160 Gleitman, Henry; Fridlund, Alan J. and Reisberg Daniel, Psychology, 6th ed., New York: Norton & Company, 2004 and Maslow, Abraham H. *The Psychology of Science*, Gateway Edition 1.95 ed., Chicago: Henry Regnery Company, 1969.

161 Abraham Harold Maslow, *The Farther Reaches of Human Nature* (New York: Viking Press, 1971), 269. (New York: Viking Press, 1971), 269.

162 "State Federation Meets," *The Montclair Times*, 1925 October 17, Start Page 1, Quote Page 2, Column 4, Montclair, New Jersey, https://www.newspapers.com/paper/the-montclair-times/11721/.

163 Joshua A. Daily and Benjamin J. Landis, "The Journey to Becoming an Adult Learner: From Dependent to Self-Directed Learning," *Journal of the American College of Cardiology* 64, no. 19 (November 11, 2014): 2066–2068, https://doi.org/10.1016/j.jacc.2014.09.023.

Bibliography

Aghababa, Aliraza, and Ali Kashi. "Effect of mindful meditation on the mindfulness state, flow state and sport performance on table tennis players." *Sport Psychology Studies* 7, no. 25 (2018): 89–110. https://doi.org/10.22089/spsyj.2018.5898.1626.

Alexandersen, Ingeborg, Hege Selnes Haugdahl, Berit Stjern, Tove Engan Paulsby, Stine Borgen Lund, and Gørill Haugan. "'I want to get back!' A qualitative study of long-term critically ill patients' inner strength and willpower: Back home after long-term intensive care." *Journal of Clinical Nursing* 30, no. 19–20 (October 2021): 3023–3035. https://pubmed.ncbi.nlm.nih.gov/34018274/.

American Heart Association. "CPR Facts & Status." CPR & First Aid Emergency Cardiovascular Care. https://cpr.heart.org/en/resources/cpr-facts-and-stats. Anderson, Mac. *Power of Attitude.* Sourcebooks, Inc., 2005.

Antiliou, G., L. Timotijevic, and M. Raats. "The role of willpower in successful maintenance of weight loss." *Psychology & Health* 27, (August 21–25, 2012): 148–149. https://openresearch.surrey.ac.uk/esploro/outputs/99516412102346?institution=44SUR_INST&skipUsageReporting=true&recordUsage=false.

Bakker, Arnold B. "Flow among music teachers and their students: The crossover of peak experiences." *Journal of Vocational Behavior* 66, no. 1 (February 2005): 26–44. https://doi.org/10.1016/j.jvb.2003.11.001. https://doi.org/10.1016/j.jvb.2003.11.001.

Barsade, Sigal G. "The Ripple Effect: Emotional Contagion and Its Influence on Group Behavior." *Administrative Science Quarterly* 47, no. 4 (December 2002): 644–675. https://doi.org/10.2307/3094912.

Benson-Greenwald, Tessa M. "The Light at the End of the Tunnel: Temporal Distancing and Academic Attitudes." PhD diss. Miami University, 2018.

Bernecker, Katharina, and Veronika Job. "Beliefs about willpower are related to therapy adherence and psychological adjustment in patients with type 2 diabetes." *Basic and Applied Social Psychology* 37, no. 3 (2015): 188–195. https://doi.org/10.1080/01973533.2015.1049348.

Boettcher, Richard E. "Interspousal Empathy, Marital Satisfaction, and Marriage Counseling." *Journal of Social Service Research* 1, no. 1 (1977): 105–113. https://doi.org/10.1300/J079v01n01_08.

Boianelli, Lynn Marie. "Achieving flow in theatre performance." Master's thesis, Rowan University, September 2, 2005.

Bostdorff, Denise M. "The internet rhetoric of the Ku Klux Klan: A case study in web site community building run amok." *Communication Studies* 55, no. 2 (2004): 340–361. https://doi.org/10.1080/10510970409388623.

Brown, Brené. *Braving the Wilderness: The Quest for True Belonging and the Courage to Stand Alone.* New York: Random House, 2017.

Brown, Bruce Eamon. *1001 Motivational Messages and Quotes for Athletes and Coaches: Teaching Character Through Sport.* Monterey, CA: Coaches Choice, 2000.

Bruehlman-Senecal, Emma, and Ozlem Ayduk. "This too shall pass: temporal distance and the regulation of emotional distress." *Journal of Personality and Social Psychology* 108, no. 2 (February 2015): 356. https://doi.org/10.1037/a0038324.

Camacho, E.M., S.M.M. Verstappen, and D.P.M. Symmons. "Association between socioeconomic status, learned helplessness, and disease outcome in patients with inflammatory polyarthritis." *Arthritis Care & Research* 64, no. 8 (March 21, 2012): 1225–1232. https://doi.org/10.1002/acr.21677.

Carhart-Harris, Robin L., Leor Roseman, Mark Bolstridge, Lysia Demetriou, J Nienke Pannekoek, Matthew B Wall, Mark Tanner et al. "Psilocybin for treatment-resistant depression: fMRI-measured brain mechanisms." *Scientific Reports* 7, no. 1 (October 13, 2017): 1–11. https://doi.org/10.1038/s41598-017-13282-7.

Castillo-Richard, A., R.H. Schneider, C.N. Alexander, R. Cook, H. Myers, S. Nidich, C. Haney, M. Rainforth, and J. Salerno. "Effects of Stress Reduction on Carotid Atherosclerosis in Hypertensive African Americans." *Stroke* 31, no. 3 (March 1, 2000): 568–573. https://doi.org/10.1161/01.STR.31.3.568.

Centers for Disease Control and Prevention, "COVID Data Tracker," US Department of Health and Human Services, CDC, accessed July 23 2022, https://COVID.cdc.gov/COVID-data-tracker.

Cesari, Matteo, Brenda W.J.H. Penninx, Anne B. Newman, Stephen B. Kritchevsky, Barbara J. Nicklas, Kim Sutton-Tyrrell, Susan M. Rubin et al. "Inflammatory markers and onset of cardiovascular events: results from the Health ABC study." *Circulation* 108, no. 19 (November 11, 2003): 2317–2322. https://pubmed.ncbi.nlm.nih.gov/14568895/.

Chamberlain, John M., and David A.F. Haaga. "Unconditional Self-Acceptance and Responses to Negative Feedback." *Journal of Rational-Emotive & Cognitive-Behavior Therapy* 19, no. 3 (September 2001): 177–189. https://doi.org/10.1023/A:1011141500670.

Chau, Danny. "What It Means to Understand Bruce Lee." *The Atlantic,* June 22 2020. https://www.theatlantic.com/culture/archive/2020/06/be-water-and-difficulty-understanding-bruce-lee/613234/.

Chen, Yi-Chun, Hsien-Ching Chiu, and Chia-Yu Chu. "Drug Reaction With Eosinophilia and Systemic Symptoms: A Retrospective Study of 60 Cases." *Archives of Dermatology* 146, no. 12 (August 2010): 1373–1379. https://jamanetwork.com/journals/jamadermatology/fullarticle/422535.

Chishima, Yuta, I-Ting Huai-Ching Liu, and Anne E. Wilson. "Temporal distancing during the COVID-19 pandemic: Letter writing with future self can mitigate negative affect." *Applied Psychology: Health and Well-Being* 13, no. 2 (May 2021): 406–418. https://doi.org/10.1111/aphw.12256.

Christensen, David, Jeff Barnes, and David Rees. "Developing Resolve to Have Moral Courage: A field Comparison of Teaching Methods." *Journal of Business Ethics Education* 4, (2007): 79–96. https://www.proquest.com/openview/4a2d8ca54a50b5b2ea29ebd181515d0d /1?pq-origsite=gscholar&cbl=307110.

Cruz, Jonas Preposi, Darren Neil C. Cabrera, Only D. Hufana, Nahed Alquwez, and Joseph Almazan. "Optimism, proactive coping and quality of life among nurses: A cross-sectional study." *Journal of Clinical Nursing* 27, no. 9–10 (March 2018): 2098–2108. https://doi.org/10.1111/ jocn.14363.

Csikszentmihályi M. *Flow: The Psychology of Optimal Experience.* New York: Harper and Row, 1990.

Daily, Joshua A., and Benjamin J. Landis. "The Journey to Becoming an Adult Learner: From Dependent to Self-Directed Learning." *Journal of the American College of Cardiology* 64, no. 19 (November 11, 2014): 2066–2068. https://doi.org/10.1016/j.jacc.2014.09.023.

De Beauvoir, Simone. *She Came to Stay: A Novel.* New York: W.W. Norton & Company, 1999.

De Beauvoir, Simone. *The Second Sex.* New York: Knopf, 2010.

Demir, Melikşah, Ömer Faruk Şimşek, and Amanda D. Procsal. "I Am so Happy 'Cause My Best Friend Makes me Feel Unique: Friendship, Personal Sense of Uniqueness and Happiness." *Journal of Happiness Studies* 14, no. 4 (2013): 1201–1224. https://doi.org/10.1007/s10902-012-9376-9.

Diener, Ed, and Martin E.P. Seligman. "Very Happy People." *Psychological Science* 13, no. 1 (January 2002): 81–84. https://doi.org/10.1111/1467-9280.00415.

Duckworth, Angela Lee, and Patrick D. Quinn. "Development and Validation of the Short Grit Scale (GRIT–S)." *Journal of Personality Assessment* 91, no. 2 (February 10, 2009): 166–174. https://doi.org/10.1080/00223890802634290.

Dudeja, Jai Paul. "Scientific Analysis of Mantra-Based Meditation and its Beneficial Effects: An Overview." *International Journal of Advanced Scientific Technologies in Engineering and Management Sciences* 3, no. 6 (June 2017): 21–26. http://www.ijastems.org/wp-content/ uploads/2017/06/v3.i6.5.Scientific-Analysis-of-Mantra-Based-Meditation.pdf.

Emerson, Ralph Waldo. *Success, Greatness, Immortality.* Boston: Houghton, Osgood and Company, 1880.

Engberg, Henriette, Bernard Jeune, Karen Andersen-Ranberg, Torben Martinussen, James W. Vaupel, and Kaare Christensen. "Optimism and survival: does an optimistic outlook predict better survival at advanced ages? A twelve-year follow-up of Danish nonagenarians." *Aging Clinical and Experimental Research* 25, no. 5 (September 7, 2013): 517–525. https://doi. org/10.1007/s40520-013-0122-x.

Ezekiel 36:25. ESV. https://biblehub.com/ezekiel/36-25.htm.

Ferrari, Madeleine, Keong Yap, Nicole Scott, Danielle A. Einstein, and Joseph Ciarrochi. "Self-compassion moderates the perfectionism and depression link in both adolescence and adulthood." *PLOS One* 13, no. 2 (February 2018): https://www.ncbi.nlm.nih.gov/pmc/articles/ PMC5821438/.

Forgeard, M.J.C., and M.E.P. Seligman. "Seeing the glass half full: A review of the causes and consequences of optimism." *Pratiques Psychologiques* 18, no. 2 (June 2012): 107–120. https://doi. org/10.1016/j.prps.2012.02.002.

Foster, J.K., G.A. Eskes, and D.T. Stuss. "The cognitive neuropsychology of attention: A frontal lobe perspective." *Cognitive Neuropsychology* 11, no. 2 (1994): 133–147. https://doi. org/10.1080/02643299408251971.

Fox, Glenn R., Jonas Kaplan, Hanna Damasio, and Antonio Damasio. "Neural correlates of gratitude." *Frontiers in Psychology* 6, (September 30, 2015): 1491. https://www.ncbi.nlm.nih.gov/pmc/articles/PMC4588123/.

Froh, Jeffrey J., William J. Sefick, and Robert A. Emmons. "Counting blessings in early adolescents: An experimental study of gratitude and subjective well-being." *Journal of School Psychology* 46, no. 2 (2008): 213-233. https://greatergood.berkeley.edu/pdfs/GratitudePDFs/3Froh-BlessingsEarlyAdolescence.pdf.

Fry, Prem S., and Dominique L. Debats. "Perfectionism and the Five-Factor Personality Traits as Predictors of Mortality in Older Adults." *Journal of Health Psychology* 14, no. 4 (May 2009): 513-524. https://pubmed.ncbi.nlm.nih.gov/19383652/.

Gallagher, Susan M. "Bullying, Moral Courage, Patient Safety, and the Bariatric Nurse." *Bariatric Nursing and Surgical Patient Care* 7, no. 4 (December 2012): 156-159. https://doi.org/10.1089/bar.2012.9954.

Gay, Simon. "Together, we are an ocean." *Education for Primary Care* 33, no. 1 (November 22, 2021): 1. https://doi.org/10.1080/14739879.2021.2005469.

Ghani, Jawaid A., and Satish P. Deshpande. "Task Characteristics and the Experience of Optimal Flow in Human—Computer Interaction." *The Journal of Psychology* 128, no. 4 (1994): 381-391, https://doi.org/10.1080/00223980.1994.9712742.

Gini, Al. "A Short Primer on Moral Courage." In Moral Courage in Organizations: Doing the Right Thing at Work, edited by Debra Comer and Gina Vega, 27-36. New York: Routledge, 2015.

Gleitman, Henry; Fridlund, Alan J. and Reisberg Daniel. Psychology. 6th ed. New York: Norton & Company, 2004 and Maslow, Abraham H. *The Psychology of Science*. Gateway Edition 1.95 ed. Chicago: Henry Regnery Company, 1969.

Greenstone, Michael, and Vishan Nigam, "Does Social Distancing Matter?" Working paper, University of Chicago, Baker Friedman Institute for Economics, 2020. https://bfi.uchicago.edu/wp-content/uploads/BFI_WP_202026.pdf.

Greyson, Bruce. "Varieties of Near-Death Experience." *Psychiatry* 56, no. 4 (November 1993): 390-399. https://med.virginia.edu/perceptual-studies/wp-content/uploads/sites/360/2017/01/NDE25.pdf.

Grover, Shawn, and John F. Helliwell. "How's Life at Home? New Evidence on Marriage and the Set Point for Happiness." *Journal of Happiness Studies: An Interdisciplinary Forum on Subjective Well-Being* 20, no. 2 (February 15, 2019): 373-390. https://doi.org/10.1007/s10902-017-9941-3.

Guttormson, Jill L., Kelly Calkins, Natalie McAndrew, Jacklynn Fitzgerald, Holly Losurdo, and Danielle Loonsfoot. "Critical Care Nurse Burnout, Moral Distress, and Mental Health During the COVID-19 Pandemic: A United States Survey." *Heart & Lung* 55 (September/October 2022): 127-133. https://www.ncbi.nlm.nih.gov/pmc/articles/PMC9050623/.

Hannah, Sean T., Bruce J. Avolio, and Fred O. Walumbwa. "Relationships between Authentic Leadership, Moral Courage, and Ethical and Pro-Social Behaviors." *Business Ethics Quarterly* 21, no. 4 (October 2011): 555-578. https://doi.org/10.5840/beq201121436.

Hanninen, T., M. Hallikainen, K. Koivisto, K. Partanen, M.P. Laakso, P.J. Riekkinen Sr., and H. Soininen. "Decline of Frontal Lobe Functions in Subjects with Age-associated Memory Impairment." *Neurology* 48, no. 1 (January 1, 1997): 148-153. https://doi.org/10.1212/WNL.48.1.148.

Hansen-Barkun, Christopher, Omar Kherad, Adamo A. Donovan, Anupa J. Prashad, and Maida J. Sewitch. "Personal protective equipment portraits in the era of COVID-19." *European Journal of Internal Medicine* 102, (May 2022): 125–127. https://doi.org/10.1016/j.ejim.2022.05.026.

Hazlett, Laura I., Mona Moieni, Michael R. Irwin, Kate E. Byrne Haltom, Ivana Jevtic, Meghan L. Meyer, Elizabeth C. Breen, Steven W. Cole, and Naomi I. Eisenberger. "Exploring neural mechanisms of the health benefits of gratitude in women: A randomized controlled trial." *Brain, Behavior, and Immunity* 95 (July 2021): 444–453. https://www.sciencedirect.com/science/article/pii/S088915912100177X.

Heine, C. "Flow and achievement in mathematics." PhD diss., University of Chicago, 1996.

Henning, Kris R., and B. Christopher Frueh. "Combat guilt and its relationship to PTSD symptoms." *Journal of Clinical Psychology* 53, no. 8 (December 8, 1997): 801–808. https://doi.org/10.1002/(SICI)1097-4679(199712)53:8<801::AID-JCLP3>3.0.CO;2-I.

Holt-Lunstad, Julianne. "The potential public health relevance of social isolation and loneliness: Prevalence, epidemiology, and risk factors." *Public Policy & Aging Report* 27, no. 4 (January 2, 2018): 127–130. https://academic.oup.com/ppar/article/27/4/127/4782506.

Holt-Lunstad, Julianne, Timothy B. Smith, Mark Baker, Tyler Harris, and David Stephenson. "Loneliness and Social Isolation as Risk Factors for Mortality." *Perspectives on Psychological Science* 10, no. 2 (March 2015): 227–237. doi:10.1177/1745691614568352.

Huberman, Andrew. "The Science of Gratitude & How to Build a Gratitude Practice." November 22, 2021, YouTube video, 1:25:56. https://youtu.be/KVjfFN89qvQ.

Institute of Medicine. *Strategies to Improve Cardiac Arrest Survival: A Time to Act.* (Washington DC: The National Academies Press, 2015). https://doi.org/10.17226/21723.

Jiang, Feng, Xiaodong Yue, Su Lu, Guangtao Yu, and Fei Zhu. "How Belief in a Just World Benefits Mental Health: The Effects of Optimism and Gratitude." *Social Indicators Research* 126, no. 1 (March 2016): 411–423. https://doi.org/10.1007/s11205-015-0877-x.

Job, Veronika, Gregory M. Walton, Katharina Bernecker, and Carol S. Dweck. "Implicit theories about willpower predict self-regulation and grades in everyday life." *Journal of Personality and Social Psychology* 108, no. 4 (2015): 637-647. https://doi.org/10.1037/pspp0000014.

Johnston, Charles. *From the Upanishads.* Portland, ME: Thomas B. Mosher, 1913.

Jordan, Alexander H., Benoît Monin, Carol S. Dweck, Benjamin J. Lovett, Oliver P. John, and James J. Gross. "Misery Has More Company Than People Think: Underestimating the Prevalence of Others' Negative Emotions." *Personality and Social Psychology Bulletin* 37, no. 1 (December 22, 2010): 120–135. https://doi.org/10.1177/0146167210390822.

Jung, Carl Gustav. "Archaic Man." In *Modern Man in Search of a Soul.* New York: Routledge, 2001. 137–164.

Kashdan, Todd B., Gitendra Uswatte, and Terri Julian. "Gratitude and hedonic and eudaimonic well-being in Vietnam war veterans." *Behaviour Research and Therapy* 44, no. 2 (February 2006): 177–199. https://pubmed.ncbi.nlm.nih.gov/16389060/.

Kassem, Suzy. *Rise Up and Salute the Sun: The Writings of Suzy Kassem.* Sedona: Awakened Press, 2011.

Katz, Jennifer, and Rebecca A. Nelson. "Family Experiences and Self-Criticism in College Students: Testing a Model of Family Stress, Past Unfairness, and Self-Esteem." *The American Journal of Family Therapy* 35, no. 5 (October 3, 2007): 447–457. https://doi.org/10.1080/01926180601057630.

Kellehear, Allan. "Culture, Biology, and the Near-Death Experience: A Reappraisal." *Journal of Nervous and Mental Disease* 181, no. 3 (March 1993): 148-156. https://journals.lww.com/jonmd/abstract/1993/03000/culture,_biology,_and_the_near_death_experience__a.2.aspx.

Kiecolt-Glaser, Janice K., and Tamara L. Newton. "Marriage and health: His and hers." *Psychological Bulletin* 127, no. 4 (July 2001): 472. https://pubmed.ncbi.nlm.nih.gov/11439708/.

Kim, Gwang-Won, Gwang-Woo Jeong, Tae-Hoon Kim, Han-Su Baek, Seok-Kyun Oh, Heoung-Keun Kang, Sam-Gyu Lee, Yoon Soo Kim, and Jin-Kyu Song. "Functional Neuroanatomy Associated with Natural and Urban Scenic Views in the Human Brain: 3.0 T Functional MR Imaging." *Korean Journal of Radiology* 11, no. 5 (August 27, 2010): 507–513. https://doi.org/10.3348/kjr.2010.11.5.507.

King Martin Luther. "Remaining Awake Through a Great Revolution." May 8, 1964, A.M.E. Church Convention, Cincinnati, OH, LP Creed Records, 1971.

Kinzler, Katherine D., and Elizabeth S. Spelke. "Do infants show social preferences for people differing in race?" *Cognition* 119, no. 1 (April 2011): 1–9. https://doi.org/10.1016/j.cognition.2010.10.019.

Kiosses, Stelios. *The Power of Talking: Stories from the Therapy Room.* Manila: Phoenix Publishing House, 2021.

Kotler, Steven. *The Rise of Superman: Decoding the Science of Ultimate Human Performance.* Boston: Houghton Mifflin Harcourt, 2014.

Kraehenmann, Rainer, Katrin H. Preller, Milan Scheidegger, Thomas Pokorny, Oliver G. Bosch, Erich Seifritz, and Franz X. Vollenweider "Psilocybin-Induced Decrease in Amygdala Reactivity Correlates with Enhanced Positive Mood in Healthy Volunteers." *Biological Psychiatry* 78, no. 8 (October 2015): 572-81. https://doi.org/10.1016/j.biopsych.2014.04.010.

Krogh-Madsen, Rikke, Peter Plomgaard, Kirsten Møller, Bettina Mittendorfer, and Bente K Pedersen. "Influence of TNF-*a* and IL-6 infusions on insulin sensitivity and expression of IL-18 in humans." *American Journal of Physiology-Endocrinology and Metabolism* 291, no. 1 (July 29, 2006): 108–114. https://pubmed.ncbi.nlm.nih.gov/16464907/#:~:text=TNF%20induced%20IL%2D18%20gene,gene%20expression%20in%20either%20tissue.

Kumar, Amit, and Nicholas Epley. "Undervaluing Gratitude: Expressers Misunderstand the Consequences of Showing Appreciation." *Psychological Science* 29, no. 9 (June 2018): 1423–1435. https://www.researchgate.net/publication/326022743_Undervaluing_Gratitude_Expressers_Misunderstand_the_Consequences_of_Showing_Appreciation.

Kweon, Byoung-Suk, Roger S. Ulrich, Verrick D. Walker, and Louis D. Tassinary. "Anger and Stress: The Role of Landscape Posters in an Office Setting." *Environment and Behavior* 40, no. 3 (2007): 355–381. https://doi.org/10.1177/0013916506298797.

Kyeong, Sunghyon, Joohan Kim, Dae Jin Kim, Hesun Erin Kim, and Jae-Jin Kim. "Effects of gratitude meditation on neural network functional connectivity and brain-heart coupling." *Scientific Reports* 7, no. 1 (July 11, 2014): 1–15. https://pubmed.ncbi.nlm.nih.gov/28698643/.

Lachman, Vicki D. "Moral courage: a virtue in need of development?." *MedSurg Nursing* 16, no. 2 (April 2007): 131. https://go.gale.com/ps/i.do?id=GALE%7CA163422064&sid=googleScholar&v=2.1&it=r&linkaccess=abs&issn=10920811&p=AONE&sw=w&userGroupName=anon%7E3fbacf26&aty=open-web-entry.

Lambert, Nathaniel M., Margaret S. Clark, Jared Durtschi, Frank D. Fincham, and Steven M. Graham. "Benefits of Expressing Gratitude: Expressing Gratitude to a Partner Changes One's View of the Relationship." *Psychological Science* 21, no. 4 (April 21, 2010): 574–580. https://pubmed.ncbi.nlm.nih.gov/20424104/.

Leigh-Hunt, N., D. Bagguley, K.Bash, V. Turner, S. Turnbull, N. Valtorta, and W. Caan. "An overview of systematic reviews on the public health consequences of social isolation and loneliness." *Public health* 152, (September 12, 2017): 157–171. https://pubmed.ncbi.nlm.nih.gov/28915435/.

Ling, Susan, Felicia Ceban, Leanna M.W. Lui, Yena Lee, Kayla M. Teopiz, Nelson B. Rodrigues, Orly Lipsitz et al. "Molecular Mechanisms of Psilocybin and Implications for the Treatment of Depression." *CNS Drugs* 36, (November 17, 2021): 1–4. https://doi.org/10.1007/s40263-021-00877-y.

Lloyd, Kasey, and William Pennington. "Towards a Theory of Minimalism and Wellbeing." *International Journal of Applied Positive Psychology* 5, no. 3 (2020): 121–136. https://doi.org/10.1007/s41042-020-00030-y.

Ma, Yunfeng, Yi Ren, Zhi-Jun Dai, Cai-Jun Wu, Yan-Hong Ji, and Jiru Xu. "IL-6, IL-8 and TNF-*a* levels correlate with disease stage in breast cancer patients." *Advances in Clinical and Experimental Medicine* 26, no. 3 (May/June 2017): 421–426. https://pubmed.ncbi.nlm.nih.gov/28791816/.

Madigan, Timothy J., and Daria Gorlova. "Aristotle on Forming Friendships." *Philosophy Now* 126 (2018): 6. https://philosophynow.org/issues/126/Aristotle_on_Forming_Friendships#:~:text=For%20Aristotle%2C%20friendships%2C%20especially%20friendships,should%20not%20be%20given%20lightly.

Maeran, Roberta, and Francesco Cangiano. "Flow experience and job characteristics: Analyzing the role of flow in job satisfaction." *TPM-Testing, Psychometrics, Methodology in Applied Psychology* 20, no. 1 (2013): 13-26. https://psycnet.apa.org/record/2013-14149-002.

Majah, Sunan Ibn. "Book of Zuhd." Vol. 5. Hadith 4259.

Martin, Leonard L., W. Keith Campbell, and Christopher D. Henry. "The Roar of Awakening: Mortality Acknowledgment as a Call to Authentic Living." In *Handbook of Experimental Existential Psychology*, edited by J. Greenberg, S.L. Koole, & T. Pyszczynski, 431–448. New York: Guilford Press, 2004.

Maslow, Abraham Harold. "Dynamics of personality organization. I." *Psychological Review* 50, no. 5 (1943): 514. https://doi.org/10.1037/h0062222.

Maslow, Abraham Harold. *The Farther Reaches of Human Nature.* 269. New York: Viking Press, 1971.

McClean, Shawn T., Joel Koopman, Junhyok Yim, and Anthony C. Klotz. "Stumbling out of the gate: The energy-based implications of morning routine disruption." *Personnel Psychology* 74, no. 3 (2021): 411–448. https://doi.org/10.1111/peps.12419.

McCrae, Niall, Sheryl Gettings, and Edward Purssell. "Social Media and Depressive Symptoms in Childhood and Adolescence: A Systematic Review." *Adolescent Research Review* 2, no. 4 (March 2, 2017): 315–330. https://link.springer.com/article/10.1007/s40894-017-0053-4.

McEvoy, Caterina. *Blue Dragon, White Tiger: The Paradox of Flux and Flow in Sound Art and Martial Arts.* PhD diss., University of Sheffield, 2019. https://etheses.whiterose.ac.uk/25751/1/PhD_Caterina%20McEvoy_Final%20Thesis%202020.pdf.

McRaven, Admiral William H. *Make Your Bed: Little Things that Can Change Your Life... and Maybe the World*. London: Hachette UK, 2017.

Mendes, Wendy Berry, Jim Blascovich, Brian Lickel, and Sarah Hunter. "Challenge and Threat During Social Interactions With White and Black Men." *Personality and Social Psychology Bulletin* 28, no. 7 (July 2002): 939–952. https://doi.org/10.1177/014616720202800707.

Mogilner, Cassie, and Michael I. Norton. "Time, money, and happiness." *Current Opinion in Psychology* 10, (2016): 12–16. https://www.hbs.edu/ris/Publication%20Files/mogilner%20norton%202016_951db108-1099-4482-8b02-27eed5e2a87e.pdf.

Montaigne. "Of Repentance." In The Complete Essays of Montaigne, edited and translated by Donald M. Frame, 614. Redwood City, CA: Stanford University Press, 1957.

Murray, Robert P., Janet J. Johnston, Jeffrey J. Dolce, Wondra Wong Lee, and Peggy O'Hara. "Social support for smoking cessation and abstinence: The lung health study." *Addictive Behaviors* 20, no. 2 (March/April 1995): 159–170. https://pubmed.ncbi.nlm.nih.gov/7484310/.

Naseem, Zarghuna, and Ruhi Khalid. "Positive Thinking in Coping with Stress and Health Outcomes: Literature Review." *Journal of Research & Reflections in Education (JRRE)* 4, no. 1 (2010) https://www.semanticscholar.org/paper/Positive-Thinking-in-Coping-with-Stress-and-Health-Naseem-Khalid/db77200dc777353a922594e868554b12e0c8448b.

Neff, Kristin D. "Self-Compassion, Self-Esteem, and Well-Being." *Social and Personality Psychology Compass* 5, no. 1 (January 2011): 1-12. https://doi.org/10.1111/j.1751-9004.2010.00330.x.

Neff, Kristin D. "The Space Between Self-Esteem and Self-Compassion." February 6, 2013, TEDx Centennial Park Women. YouTube video, 19:00, https://www.youtube.com/watch?v=IvtZBUSplr4.

Neff, Kristin D., and Katie A. Dahm. "Self-Compassion: What It Is, What It Does, and How It Relates To Mindfulness." In Handbook of Mindfulness and Self-Regulation. 121–137. Springer, New York, NY, 2015.

Neff, Kristin D., Kristin L. Kirkpatrick, and Stephanie S. Rude. "Self-compassion and adaptive psychological functioning." *Journal of Research in Personality* 41, no. 1 (2007): 139–154. https://doi.org/10.1016/j.jrp.2006.03.004.

Neff, Kristin D., Stephanie S. Rude, and Kristin L. Kirkpatrick. "An examination of self-compassion in relation to positive psychological functioning and personality traits." *Journal of research in personality* 41, no. 4 (2007): 908–916. doi:10.1016/j.jrp.2006.08.002.

Nichols, Wallace J. *Blue Mind: The Surprising Science that Shows how Being Near, In, On, or Under Water Can Make You Happier, Healthier, More Connected, and Better at What You Do*. Boston: Little, Brown and Company, 2014.

Aristotle. *Nicomachean Ethics*. Indianapolis: Hackett Publishing, 2019.

Norsworthy, Cameron, Paul Gorczynski, and Susan A. Jackson. "A systematic review of flow training on flow states and performance in elite athletes." *Graduate Journal of Sport, Exercise & Physical Education Research* 6, no. 2 (2017): 16–28. https://www.researchgate.net/profile/Cameron-Norsworthy/publication/322676172_A_SYSTEMATIC_REVIEW_OF_FLOW_TRAINING_ON_FLOW_STATES_AND_PERFORMANCE_IN_ELITE_ATHLETES/links/5e6726b5a6fdcc37dd15e0e0/A-SYSTEMATIC-REVIEW-OF-FLOW-TRAINING-ON-FLOW-STATES-AND-PERFORMANCE-IN-ELITE-ATHLETES.pdf.

Nutt, David, and Robin Carhart-Harris. "The Current Status of Psychedelics in Psychiatry." *JAMA Psychiatry* 78, no. 2 (2021): 121–122. doi:10.1001/jamapsychiatry.2020.2171.

Oettingen, Gabriele, and Thomas A. Wadden. "Expectation, fantasy, and weight loss: Is the impact of positive thinking always positive?," *Cognitive Therapy and Research* 15, no. 2 (1991): 167-175. https://doi.org/10.1007/BF01173206.

Øverup, Camilla S., Julie A. Brunson, Mai-Ly N. Steers, and Linda K. Acitelli. "I know I have to earn your love: how the family environment shapes feelings of worthiness of love." *International Journal of Adolescence and Youth* 22, no. 1 (January 28, 2014): 16–35. https://doi.org/10.1080/0 2673843.2013.868362.

Owens, J.E., Emily W. Cook, and Ian Stevenson. "Features of 'near-death experience' in relation to whether or not patients were near death." *The Lancet* 336, no. 8724 (November 10, 1990): 1175–1177. https://doi.org/10.1016/0140-6736(90)92780-L.

Page-Gould, E.. "The Unhealthy Racist." In *Are We Born Racist?*, eds. Jason Marsh, Roldolfo Mendoza-Denton, and Jeremy Adam Smith, 41–44. Boston: Beacon Press, 2010.

Page-Gould, Elizabeth, Roldolfo Mendoza-Denton, Jan Marie Alegre, and John Oliver Siy. "Understanding the impact of cross-group friendship on interactions with novel outgroup members." *Journal of Personality and Social Psychology* 98, no. 5 (2010): 775.

Parnia, Sam, and Peter Fenwick. "Near death experiences in cardiac arrest: visions of a dying brain or visions of a new science of consciousness." *Resuscitation* 52, no. 1 (January 2002): 5–11. https://doi.org/10.1016/S0300-9572(01)00469-5.

Parnia, Sam, Ken Spearpoint, and Peter B. Fenwick. "Near death experiences, cognitive function and psychological outcomes of surviving cardiac arrest." *Resuscitation* 74, no. 2 (August 2007): 215–221.

Pelham, Brett W., and William B. Swann. "From self-conceptions to self-worth: On the sources and structure of global self-esteem." *Journal of Personality and Social Psychology* 57, no. 4 (1989): 672.

Plato. *The Symposium.* Translated by Frisbee C.C. Sheffield. Cambridge: Cambridge University Press, 2008.

Pompeii. "New victims from Pompeii emerge from the excavation of the House of the Chaste Lovers." Accessed July 7, 2023. http://pompeiisites.org/en/comunicati/new-victims-from-pompeii-emerge-from-the-excavation-of-the-house-of-the-chaste-lovers/.

Quran, 21–30.

Reber, Kelseyleigh. *If I Fall.* New York: Aperture Press, 2013.

Rippe, James M. "Lifestyle Medicine: The Health Promoting Power of Daily Habits and Practices." *American Journal of Lifestyle Medicine* 12, no. 6 (November/December 2018): 499–512. https://doi.org/10.1177/1559827618785554.

Roberts, Steven O., and Michael T. Rizzo. "The Psychology of American Racism." *American Psychologist* 76, no. 3 (2021): 475. doi: 10.1037/amp0000642.

Rosenberg, Larry. "The Supreme Meditation." *Lion's Roar* (September 15, 2020). https://www.lionsroar.com/the-supreme-meditation/.

Ross, Loretta J. "Speaking up without tearing down." *Learning for Justice 61, (Spring 2019).* https://www.learningforjustice.org/magazine/spring-2019/speaking-up-without-tearing-down.

Ross, S., M. Agrawal, R.R. Griffiths, C. Grob, A. Berger, and J.E. Henningfield. "Psychedelic-assisted psychotherapy to treat psychiatric and existential distress in life-threatening medical illnesses and palliative care." *Neuropharmacology* 216, (September 15, 2022): 109174. https://doi.org/10.1016/j.neuropharm.2022.109174.

Roth, Gregory A., Sophia Emmons-Bell, Heather M. Alger, Steven M. Bradley, Sandeep R. Das, James A. de Lemos, Emmanuela Gakidou et al. "Trends in Patient Characteristics and COVID-19 In-Hospital Mortality in the United States During the COVID-19 Pandemic." *JAMA Network Open* 4, no. 5 (May 2021). https://www.ncbi.nlm.nih.gov/pmc/articles/PMC8094014/.

Rumi, Mevlana Jalaluddin. *Love's Ripening: Rumi on the Heart's Journey.* Boulder: Shambhala Publications, 2008.

Russell, Robin J.H., and Pamela A. Wells. "Predictors of happiness in married couples." *Personality and Individual Differences* 17, no. 3 (September 1994): 313–321. https://doi.org/10.1016/0191-8869(94)90279-8.

Sarton, May. *Journal of a Solitude.* Issue 853. New York: W.W. Norton & Company, 1992.

Seneca, Lucius Annaeus. *On the Shortness of Life.* Vol. 1. London: Penguin UK, 2004.

Setlack, Jennifer. "Workplace Violence and Mental Health of Paramedics and Firefighters." Master's Thesis, University of Manitoba, 2019. https://mspace.lib.umanitoba.ca/items/149f5c7c-c8d3-4a01-8ed8-cd3e4bcfbe6c.

Seyfarth, Robert M., and Dorothy L. Cheney. "The Evolutionary Origins of Friendship." *Annual Review of Psychology* 63 (July 5, 2011): 153–177. https://pubmed.ncbi.nlm.nih.gov/21740224/.

Solomon, Steven. *Water: The Epic Struggle for Wealth, Power, and Civilization.* HarperCollins, 2010.

Stan, Amelia Elena. "Psychological effects of aquatic activity in hydrotherapy programs." *Marathon* 5, no. 2 (2013): 205–209. https://doi.org/10.3389/fpsyt.2022.1051551.

"State Federation Meets." *The Montclair Times.* October 17, 1925. Start Page 1, Quote Page 2, Column 4. Montclair, New Jersey. https://www.newspapers.com/paper/the-montclair-times/11721/.

Thompson, Brian L., and Jennifer A. Waltz. "Mindfulness, self-esteem, and unconditional self-acceptance." *Journal of Rational-Emotive & Cognitive-Behavior Therapy* 26, no. 2 (2008): 119--126. https://doi.org/10.1007/s10942-007-0059-0.

Tirmidhi, Muhammad I. Jami' Al-Tirmidhi. Karachi: Karkhana Tijarat Kutab. (1900).

Tobin, Martin J., and Karl Yang. "Weaning from Mechanical Ventilation." *Critical Care Clinics* 6, no. 3 (July 1990): 725–747.

Twenge, Jean M. Generation Me—*Revised and Updated: Why Today's Young Americans are More Confident, Assertive, Entitled—and More Miserable Than Ever Before.* New York: Simon & Schuster, 2014.

Umberson, Debra. "Gender, marital status and the social control of health behavior." *Social Science & Medicine* 34, no. 8 (April 1992): 907–917. https://pubmed.ncbi.nlm.nih.gov/1604380/.

Valtorta, Nicole K., Mona Kanaan, Simon Gilbody, Sara Ronzi, and Barbara Hanratty. "Loneliness and social isolation as risk factors for coronary heart disease and stroke: systematic review and meta-analysis of longitudinal observational studies." *Heart* 102, no. 13 (April 18, 2016): 1009–1016. https://pubmed.ncbi.nlm.nih.gov/27091846/.

van den Bos, Kees. "Meaning making following activation of the behavioral inhibition system: How caring less about what others think may help us to make sense of what is going on." In *The Psychology of Meaning,* edited by K.D. Markman, T. Proulx, and M.J. Lindberg. 359–380. Washington DC, American Psychological Association, 2013. https://doi.org/10.1037/14040-018.

Van Lommel, P., Meyers V. Wees Van R, and I. Elfferich. "The Merkawah Research on Near Death Experience: A prospective study of 344 survivors of cardiac arrest." *The Lancet* (2001).

Wahbeh, Helané, Amira Sagher, Wallis Back, Pooja Pundhir, and Frederick Travis. "A Systematic Review of Transcendent States Across Meditation and Contemplative Traditions." *Explore* 14, no. 1 (January/February 2018): 19–35. https://doi.org/10.1016/j.explore.2017.07.007.

Waite, Sue. "'Memories are made of this': Some reflections on outdoor learning and recall." *Education 3–13* 35, no. 4 (2007): 333–347. https://doi.org/10.1080/03004270701602459.

Walton, Kenneth G., Jeremy Z. Fields, Debra K. Levitsky, Dwight A. Harris, Nirmal D. Pugh, and Robert H. Schneider. "Lowering Cortisol and CVD Risk in Postmenopausal Women: A Pilot Study Using the Transcendental Meditation Program." *Annals of the New York Academy of Sciences* 1032, no. 1 (December 2004): 211-215. https://doi.org/10.1196/annals.1314.023.

Warren, Ricks, Elke Smeets, and Kristin Neff. "Self-criticism and self-compassion: risk and resilience: being compassionate to oneself is associated with emotional resilience and psychological well-being." *Current Psychiatry* 15, no. 12 (December 2016): 18–28. https://self-compassion.org/wp-content/uploads/2016/12/Self-Criticism.pdf.

Seneca. "Letter 52." In Moral Letters to Lucilius. Translated by Richard Mott Gummere. London: William Heinemann, 1917/1920/1925. https://en.wikisource.org/wiki/Moral_letters_to_Lucilius/Letter_52

Winter, Tim J. "The Muslim grand narrative." In *Caring for Muslim Patients*. 2nd edition. Edited by Sheikh A., Gatrad AR, 25–34. Oxon: Radcliffe Publishing Ltd, 2008.

Wong, Paul T.P. "Meaning management theory and death acceptance." In *Existential and Spiritual Issues in Death Attitudes*. 91–114. New York: Psychology Press, 2007. https://www.taylorfrancis.com/chapters/edit/10.4324/9780203809679-10/meaning-management-theory-death-acceptance-paul-wong.

Wood, Alex M., Stephen Joseph, and John Maltby. "Gratitude predicts psychological well-being above the Big Five facets." *Personality and Individual Differences* 46, no. 4 (March 2009): 443–447. https://www.sciencedirect.com/science/article/abs/pii/S019188690800425X.

Yadav, Sheetal, and S.K. Srivastava. "A study of marital satisfaction and happiness among love married couples and arrange married couples." *International Review of Social Sciences and Humanities* 9, no. 8 (August 2019): 1–9. https://doi.org/10.1016/j.ssresearch.2012.09.002.

Yan, Shijiao, Yong Gan, Nan Jiang, Rixing Wang, Yunqiang Chen, Zhiqian Luo, Qiao Zong, Song Chen, and Chuanzhu Lv. "The global survival rate among adult out-of-hospital cardiac arrest patients who received cardiopulmonary resuscitation: A systematic review and meta-analysis." *Critical Care* 24, no. 61 (February 22, 2020). https://doi.org/10.1186/s13054-020-2773-2.

Young, Kevin P., Diana L. Kolcz, David M. O'Sullivan, Jennifer Ferrand, Jeremy Fried, and Kenneth Robinson. "Health Care Workers' Mental Health and Quality of Life During COVID-19: Results From a Mid-Pandemic, National Survey." *Psychiatric Services* 72, no. 2 (December 3, 2020): 122–128. https://doi.org/10.1176/appi.ps.202000424.

Yu, Hongbo, Qiang Cai, Bo Shen, Xiaoxue Gao, and Xiaolin Zhou. "Neural substrates and social consequences of interpersonal gratitude: Intention matters." *Emotion* 17, no. 4 (June 2017): 589. https://pubmed.ncbi.nlm.nih.gov/27936814/.

Zoch, Thomas W., Norman A. Desbiens, Frank DeStefano, Dean T. Stueland, and Peter M. Layde. "Short- and Long-term Survival After Cardiopulmonary Resuscitation." *Arch Intern Med.* 160, no. 13 (January 6, 2000): 1969–1973. doi:10.1001/archinte.160.13.1969.

Zumbrunnen, John. " 'Courage in the Face of Reality': Nietzsche's Admiration for Thucydides." *Polity* 35, no. 2 (2002): 237–263. https://www.journals.uchicago.edu/doi/abs/10.1086/POLv35n2ms3235499#:~:text=Abstract,explore%20Nietzsche's%20admiration%20for%20Thucydides.

Printed in the USA
CPSIA information can be obtained
at www.ICGtesting.com
LVHW042144150924
790969LV00007B/328/J